Fortify Your Data:
A Guide to the Emerging Technologies

Michael Hudak

Contents

Introduction:
Why is Data Important?

Why is Data Important?

Before we can truly speak to how to secure it, let's talk about why you should secure it.

Data is another word for information. Data is your information, your customer's information, your competitor's information, and all information in between – but even though data is just another word for information, it is special. It is special because when techies refer to it, they typically are referring to the information that is interpreted by machines and computers rather than the information interpreted by humans.

You see, this particular computer interpreted information is extremely valuable because it is your company's trade secrets, your customer's information, your employee's personal information, and everything in between. If those types of information were not valuable, then there would be no such thing as a 'hacker'. After all, why would you try to hack or steal something if you wouldn't gain value?

Nefarious entities today can steal customer information to sell to criminals that conduct vote fraud on a massive scale. They can take your entire company's email server and hold it hostage with ransomware and charge you millions to get your business operational again. They can steal your server's processing power and use it to mine cryptocurrency in the background, causing your servers to crash and your electric bill to go up.

Data is important because it is the currency of technology, and today every business is a technology company. Regardless of what your business does, the fact remains the same – business runs on tech.

In the present, many technology evangelists frame the solutions they market around data. Whether it is about protecting your data, analyzing your data, mining your data… the market today views data as paramount. That's also why I've written a book about data (the one you are currently reading), because data is pretty darn important.

Part 1
Cybersecurity

Chapter 1
An Introduction to Cybersecurity

So, What Exactly is Cybersecurity?

Cybersecurity is a tech term often associated with and used in the computer field that gets thrown around quite a bit. The analogy is not fortuitous. Cybersecurity is security of all things cyber. But what is cybersecurity really? What are the mechanisms, the foundations and especially how does this translate into our daily personal and professional lives?

Cybersecurity is a set of technologies, processes, and practices that are designed to protect networks, computers, and data from unauthorized attacks, damage, and access. In an information technology context, the term "security" includes cybersecurity and physical security. That means that hackers can come in through the internet *and* through the front door of your workplace.

Cybersecurity seeks to ensure that the security properties of organizations, and its users assets, are not only maintained but maintained in relation to security risks in the cyber environment.

Cybersecurity also means the implementation of measures to protect systems, networks and software applications from digital attacks. Such attacks are usually aimed at gaining access to confidential information, its modification and destruction, at extorting money from users or at disrupting the normal operation of companies.

Implementing effective cybersecurity measures is currently quite a challenge, since today there are far more devices than people, and attackers are becoming more and more inventive.

To ensure cybersecurity, coordinated efforts are required across the information system. Cybersecurity includes (but is not necessarily limited to):

- application security

- information security

- network security

- disaster recovery / business continuity

- operational security

- end user awareness

One of the most problematic aspects of cybersecurity is the constant and rapid evolution of security risks. The traditional approach used to be to focus most of the resources available on critical system components and protect them against the major known threats. This meant leaving some important systems defenseless and giving up the fight against some less important risks. In the current context, this approach is no longer sufficient. Adam Vincent is Technical Director for the Public Sector at Layer 7 Technologies, a security services company that works for US federal services, including some of the Department of Defense services. He explains:

"The threats evolve too fast so we have time to follow them. They change our perception of the notion of risk. Today, it is no longer possible to write a white paper on a risk for a particular system, it should be rewritten permanently ... ".

To cope with the current environment, consulting firms recommend a more proactive, adaptive approach. For example, the National Institute of Standards and Technology (NIST) has just released an update of its recommendations on the risk assessment framework, which recommends real-time assessments and ongoing monitoring.

Forbes estimated the global cyber security market at $ 75 billion in 2015 and predicts it will reach $ 170 billion in 2020.

What are the principles underlying cyber security?

A successful cybersecurity approach is expressed in the form of multilevel protection covering computers, networks, programs or data that must be secured. Employees, workflows, and technology must complement each other in organizations to provide effective protection against cyber-attacks.

Employees

Users should understand and follow basic information security principles, such as choosing strong passwords, paying attention to attachments in emails, and backing up data. Additional information on basic cybersecurity principles.

Processes

The organization should develop a set of basic measures to counter ongoing and successfully carried out attacks. You can be guided by one reliable set of measures. This set of measures should explain how to identify attacks, protect systems, identify and counter threats, and recover from the attacks. Watch a video clip with explanations about the NIST cybersecurity solution package.

Technology

Technologies are an essential element, providing organizations and individual users with the tools they need to protect against cyber-attacks. The main components that need to be protected are endpoints, such as computers, smart devices and routers; network and cloud environment. The most common technologies used to protect the listed components include new-generation firewalls, DNS filtering, malware protection, antivirus software, and email protection solutions.

Why is cybersecurity so important?

In the modern "connected" world, extended cyber defense programs serve the benefit of each user. At the individual level, cyber defense burglary can lead to a variety of consequences, ranging from theft of personal information to extortion of money or loss of valuable data, such as family photos. All depend on critical infrastructure, such as power plants, hospitals, and financial services companies. The protection of these and other organizations is important for the maintenance of our society.

Everyone benefits from the cyber threat research that cyber threat specialists are engaged in. Cybersecurity analysts and technicians studying new and emerging threats, as well as cyber-attack strategies around the world collaborate and share information discovered about new threats. They reveal new vulnerabilities, inform the public about the importance of cybersecurity, and increase the reliability of open source tools. The work of these specialists makes the Internet more secure for each user.

Every year massive amounts of funds are spent on cybersecurity, and the annual increase in spending is more than 5 times higher than the increase in funds spent in the IT sphere as a whole. With an accumulated annual growth rate estimated at 8.3% by 2020 ($ 3.8 trillion) compared with 0.9% in 2016 ($ 3.4 trillion). However, money aimed at developing and ensuring cybersecurity does not affect the greatest threat: human users. About 95% of all information leakages are related to the human factor.

With the increasing diversity of cyber threats, the number of decisions is growing, however, fatigue from constant news and warnings about the dangers of new threats may affect the current state of affairs. "There is a form of growing desensitization to daily reports on cyber-attacks and threats, to the point where some are beginning to wonder: what's the meaning of cyber security?" Said Earl Perkins, vice president of digital security gurus.

Fortunately, well-designed security procedures, methods, and solutions can almost completely stop intruders. But this requires the joint efforts of professionals, employees, partners, and customers to minimize all types of attacks and control so that problems do not turn into a catastrophe.

Chapter 2
Understanding
Cybersecurity Attacks

DDoS attack

A distributed denial of service attack - or DDoS (Distributed Denial of Service) - is a simultaneous and massive sending of information requests to a central server. The attacker forms such requests with the help of a large number of compromised systems.

By acting in a similar way, an attacker seeks to expend Internet connection resources and RAM on the system under attack. The ultimate goal is to disable the target system and damage the company.

What is the purpose of DDoS attacks?

The attacker can use a DDoS attack to extort money from the company. DDoS attacks can also benefit a company's competitors, or political dividends to governments or "hacker activists." Failure of the network infrastructure can be beneficial to many people.

What can be the duration of DDoS attacks?

The duration of DDoS attacks may vary. The Ping of Death (Ping of Death) attack can be short-lived. A longer period of time is required to implement a Slowloris attack. is a type of <u>denial of service</u> attack tool invented by Robert «RSnake" Hansen which allows a single machine to take down another machine's web server with minimal bandwidth and side effects on unrelated services and ports. According to a Radware report, 33 percent of DDoS attacks last less than one hour, 60 percent of attacks last less than a day, and 15 percent of attacks take about one month.

What measures are taken to protect against DDoS attacks?

Protecting companies from DDoS attacks is an essential element of network security. To protect your network infrastructure from a wide range of attacks, you need to be guided by an integrated and holistic IT approach that uses components that work together effectively.

The 3 most common types of DDoS attacks

Exhaustion Attacks

UDP Packet Saturation Attack: The UDP Packet Attack is conducted on randomly selected ports of the remote server using queries called UDP packets. The host checks the ports for the presence of relevant applications. If the application cannot be found, the system sends a "recipient unavailable" packet in response to each request. Traffic generated by this may exceed network resources.

ICMP saturation attack (echo requests): an attack with a saturation of packets using the ICMP protocol sends echo request packets to the host ("pings") to the host. Pings are commonly used to verify communication between two servers. After sending the ping, the server responds to it immediately. When attacking with echo requests, the attacker uses an excessive number of requests to exhaust the bandwidth in the incoming and outgoing directions on the target server.

Attacks at the application level

HTTP packet saturation attack: HTTP packet saturation attacks are carried out at Layer 7, corresponding to applications, and botnets are used, often referred to as the "army of zombies." This type of attack saturates the resources of the web server or application using standard GET and POST requests. The server is overflowing with requests and may stop working. These attacks are particularly difficult to detect, since they look like completely normal traffic.

Attack of the Slowloris type: denoted by the name of the primate "Fat Lory" (Slowloris), which is found in Asia and moves very slowly. With this attack, small parts of HTTP requests are sent to the server. These parts are sent at regular intervals so that the corresponding period of waiting for the request does not expire, and the server waits for it to be fully received. Such incomplete requests consume bandwidth and affect the ability of the server to process legitimate requests.

Protocol-level attacks

SYN Overflow Attack: In a SYN Overflow Attack, the attacker sends outwardly normal SYN requests to the server, which responds by sending a SYN-ACK request (synchronization acknowledgment). Under normal circumstances, the client then sends an ACK request, and a network connection is established. But with a SYN overflow attack, the attacker does not send the last ACK request. The server is in a situation with a large number of pending SYN-ACK requests that create a large load on the system.

Ping of Death (Ping of Death) attack: when a Ping of Death (Ping of Death) attack is launched, an attacker attempts to disable or stop the server's operation by sending echo requests that are either fragmented or unnecessarily big size. The standard IPv4 header size is 65,535 bytes. When sending a larger ping request, the target server is forced to divide the file into fragments. Then, when the server generates a response and assembles this large file, a buffer overflow may occur and the system will fail.

Attacks Drive-by download

Drive-by Download attacks consist of a program that is automatically downloaded to your computer without your consent or even with knowledge but with ignorance.

Drive-by Download attacks are triggered simply when a victim clicks on a link that inadvertently injects malicious software into the computer or other device. The most frequently used malware in Drive-by Download attacks are called Trojan viruses, named after the mythical Trojan horse story where the Greeks offered Troy a massive horse statue as a gift, however this gift was filled with Greek warriors ready to ambush the city. Like the Trojan horse, a Trojan virus is not a great gift to receive.

Statistics

Cybercriminals prefer to use well-established, high-traffic websites as targets to carry out their attacks. According to a 2012 study conducted by Barracuda Labs, more than 50% of all sites offering drive-by downloads were more than five years old.

How to defend against drive-by download attacks?

Encourage employees to keep their software updated or enforce it. The most important measure so that IT departments can be protected from bad direct downloads is to encourage employees to keep all their software updated, especially their antivirus software, their browsers and all their downloads. Add-ons including Java, Flash and Adobe Acrobat, all without centralized control or update policies within the company are security risks that should be monitored.

Ensuring that employees are using the latest versions of their browsers and extensions is critical as many employees run some previous versions.

Install web filtering software or proxies

Web filtering products can prevent people from accessing sites compromised by direct downloads. They can have built-in mechanisms that allow them to detect if a site is not secure, and if so, prevent users from going there. Some search for known exploits and known indicators of drive-by downloads, while others have built-in heuristics that help determine if a site is safe.

Install NoScript in the Firefox browser

NoScript is a free open source add-on that allows only trusted websites to run JavaScript, Java and Flash. Brandt says that running Firefox with NoScript prevents "many" drive-by downloads. As far as I can tell, it is the only infallible method to prevent accidental infection of a Windows PC by manipulated web pages.

Disable Java

Disabling JavaScript within the PDF documents in the preferences closes a door for malicious software to infiltrate your browser. It is also recommended that IT departments uninstall Java from any system exposed to a malicious Java applet stored inside a Java Archive file that allows an unsigned applet to potentially have unlimited access to execute arbitrary Java code.

Keep the tabs in BLADE

BLADE, which stands for Block All Drive-By Download Exploits, is an emerging Windows immunization system that prevents drive-by exploits from infecting vulnerable Windows machines. It is being developed by Georgia Tech researchers and will soon be available for download.

Do not grant users administrator access to the pcs. When supplying pcs to end users, employees with standard user accounts are created, they do not give end users local administrative access to their computers.

Limiting administrative access by end users to the computer mitigates the damage that malware can cause, although this practice is debatable.

Phishing attacks

Phishing attacks are the main vector of malware attacks and are usually composed of a malicious email attachment or an email with an embedded and malicious link. Phishing emails, in general, falsely claim that they are an established or legitimate business.

Phishing emails are usually easy to detect if you know what you are looking for. They often have a large number of grammatical and spelling errors and tend to request personal or credit information. In addition to that, it usually comes from a source that normally does not require this information, it already has the information or it does not usually direct the user towards external links by email.

There are 7 types of recognized phishing attacks:

- Phishing websites

- Attacks on social networks

- Spear-Phishing

- Fraudulent tax returns

- Calls tlf. Phishy

- Charity Phishing

- CEO Phishing

Recent cases of phishing

A new sophisticated espionage campaign targeting NATO governments with documents specially designed to deliver Flash exploits has been one of the last phishing campaigns this year. The campaign began during the Christmas and New Year holidays, the hackers used a Word document titled "Declaration of the Secretary General of NATO after a meeting of the NATO-Russia Council" as a bait of deception.

Where the attacks aim to perform a recognition activity in the systems. The attack was so sophisticated that researchers dubbed the "Matryoshka Doll Reconnaissance Framework".

The content of the document has been copied from an official NATO statement published on its website and the RTF file does not contain any exploits, both circumstances make it difficult for the victims to detect the attack.

The malicious document contains a sequence of embedded objects, including OLE objects and Adobe Flash, that are extracted in a specific order.

"The OLE object contains an Adobe Flash object; the goal of Adobe Flash is to extract a binary blob embedded in itself through the execution of ActionScript." "This blob is a second compressed and compressed Adobe Flash object, the encoded algorithm is based on XOR and zlib compression, this is the second Adobe Flash on the final payload that is inside the document."

The payload analysis revealed that its most relevant component is in the ActionScript code. The first ActionScript action is to contact a specific URL.

In this way, the attacker collects information about the target, including the version of the operating system or the version of Adobe Flash that is used to evaluate the chances of success of attacking the machine or not.

The data collected can allow the attacker to determine if the infected system is a sandbox or a virtual machine and stop the operations that are executed in it.

At this point, the malicious code makes two additional nested requests that use the data obtained from the response to the previous request, where, finally, in the final phase of the attack, a Flash exploit is searched, decoded and executed.

The APWG (Anti-Phishing Working Group) reported that the number of phishing websites increased by 250% between October 2015 and March 2016.

According to Verizon, 30% of phishing messages are opened by specific users and 12% of those users click on the malicious attachment or link.

Spear-phishing attacks

Spear-phishing is the fraudulent practice of sending emails ostensibly from a known or trusted sender to induce specific people to reveal confidential information.

The Spear phishing attack is among the most popular entry points for cybersecurity infractions. A spear phishing attack requires advanced hacking skills and is very difficult to detect because they generally depend on the end user opening a file in a personal and specific email. Spear phishing attacks are usually directed at decision-makers within a company. Often pretending to be a trusted colleague, a friend or an associated company, owners, managers and administrators must be fully trained and aware of the "tactics" in these cleverly malicious messages.

It is commented that the inflations of Yahoo began with a spear-phising as an attack factor.

A few months ago, a new filtration of 32 million accounts, which would join two attacks recognized in recent years: one of more than one billion accounts and another of 500 million accounts, in 2013 and 2014, has been revealed again. According to The Next Web, an investigation carried out by the US Securities and Exchange Commission (SEC) has discovered that more than 32 million Yahoo accounts were leaked.

In an interview with Ars Technica, FBI agent Malcolm Palmore said hackers could use a "spear phishing" email to obtain the credentials of Yahoo employees. Spear phishing emails can include several techniques designed to trick the recipient into giving up their personal information. Generally, phishing emails seem to come from a reliable source.

Statistics

- According to a Trend Micro report, 91% of cyber-attacks are initiated by an email spear phishing.

- SANS Institute reports that 95% of all corporate network attacks are the result of successful spear phishing.

- Intel Reports, 97% of people around the world cannot identify an attack using a sophisticated phishing email.

How to defend against a phishing attack?

Given the danger of opening a spear phishing email, it is important to keep users informed and attentive. Here are some tips and best practices to convey that can help protect them from spear phishing:

Check twice before clicking

Users should be reminded to stop before clicking the links in an email and place the cursor over the hyperlink to see the destination URL first. Spear phishers often hide their URLs in the text of the email with things like "click here to confirm" or "we just need more information, fill in this form" to have someone click without thinking. When the linked text is passed, the URL to which the link points will be displayed. If it is not familiar, do not click.

Verify the sender

One of the favorite tactics of phishing is to find a list of executives in a company and send emails imitating those executives for employees to reveal sensitive information. We must remind users that if they receive an email with a request that seems out of the ordinary, no matter who it is, they should check with the sender to confirm that it is legitimate. If that person says he did not send an email, then the problem should be reported to the CSIRT immediately.

Never send confidential information by email

Very often, phishing sends emails to employees and requests confidential information, such as user passwords or corporate banking information. Sending this information by email is never a good idea. Make sure that users notify you to let you know if someone makes these types of requests, as it is an indication that your company may be the target of phishing attacks.

Avoid publishing too much personal information online

A key part of a phisher's strategy is to use online the personal information they discover about their possible objectives. We must remind your users that publishing too much personal information publicly can help attackers cheat and break the security of the company. We must be especially careful.

Use an endpoint protection based on behavior

While there are many things you can do to help keep your users safe, no strategy, tool or behavior will be effective 100% of the time. Sooner or later, someone will click on something that will open a gap. The use of an endpoint protection tool based on behavior will help to ensure that, if something is fixed, malware infection can be detected and stopped before it causes any damage.

Given the potential gains that cybercriminals can get from spear phishing, it seems likely that it will become a bigger problem.

However, with the right tools, training and strategy, you can keep your users and your company safe.

Network probe attacks

Network-probes attacks consist in the placement of a network probe as an attempt to gain access to a computer and its files through a known or probable weak point in computer systems.

Network probes are not an immediate threat. However, they do indicate that someone is installing their system for possible entry points as a vector for the attack. Basically, it is a network monitor that analyzes protocols and network traffic in real time.

How to defend against Network probes attacks?

Once a thorough understanding has been recorded and the events of the probe have been recorded, management and the security team should be alerted about the probe so that they can perform a forensic analysis and make executive decisions on how to proceed, coordinating everything from the CSIRT. Once informed, we must continue to monitor the activity by placing additional intrusion detection sensors in the discovered sections of the network and take advantage of the operations center, and try to determine what was most striking in the first place, helping prevent future occurrences.

Brute force attacks

Brute force and Cracking attacks are a trial and error method used by application programs to decode encrypted data such as passwords or data encryption keys (DES), by exhaustive effort (using brute force) instead of using intellectual or more sophisticated strategies.

Cracking brute force basically means continually injecting a password until one does it right, allowing entry to the site being attacked.

Similar means of trial and error are also mediated by a similar tactic to find hidden pages within the websites.

Recent cases

Researchers at the Preempt behavior firewall company have analyzed leaked LinkedIn passwords to find out how many were weak before the breach occurred.

Findings show that 35 percent of filtered LinkedIn passwords, more than 63 million and a half, were already known by previous passwords dictionaries, making them vulnerable to decryption without connection by reference to a list of words of known or used passwords previously.

In addition, 65 percent could be easily broken with brute force using standard commercial cracking hardware.

All this means that the conventional techniques of using uppercase and lowercase characters, symbols and digits (ULSD) to create passwords are less effective. Partly because users re-use passwords, but also because they rotate them, for example, by adding digits at the end.

Anyone who uses the same password for LinkedIn as for their work or another account is vulnerable within these other accounts. Unfortunately, many users do not make that connection. Knowing that LinkedIn was violated, they only change their LinkedIn password, without realizing that if they are using that same password elsewhere, they are also exposed in all those places. For IT security teams, this is an additional vulnerability that they have to deal with.

According to the research, low-complexity 10-character passwords, where only the length is applied, can be divided in less than a day using standard hardware. Passwords of average complexity with common ULSD patterns, for example, a main case and a final number, can be deciphered in less than a week. High complexity passwords that do not use common patterns can take up to a month to decrypt.

In 2016, brute force attacks more than doubled in the space of two months. WordPress had especially high levels of brute force attacks.

With the increase in technological advancements in cyber defense, cybercrime has been given additional tools to carry out their operations. Stronger and stronger processors and computer resources make brute force attacks on networks much easier to carry out.

How to defend against brute force attacks?

When it comes to Windows, authentication mode and privacy lock settings are an easy and effective way to avoid brute-force attack attempts, since they make the attack slower.

It is important to never use a domain administrator account as a SQL database connection account, as it could lead from a brute force attack to a denial of service condition.

The vulnerability for brute force attack of SQL servers lacks functions that detect systems under a brute force attack, which makes it a completely new and very dangerous beast. It is a very difficult task to protect an application that requires administrative privileges at the domain level and lacks the ability to execute in an earlier version of SQL Server, being able to see the encryption of the database connection, as well as the way in which connects and authenticates in the application. Each database and application system are a bit different and require variations of precautionary measures.

But as a better defense, the second authentication factor, abbreviated 2FA, is, as the name suggests, a method to verify that the person who is trying to access an account is its real owner and not someone who knows his or her password. Let's take a very simple example. To access our house, we use a key, but when we go to sleep, we usually put a latch in case someone has copied the key. The second factor is that latch on the Internet.

In this way, if someone knows our password, they will not be able to access our accounts if they do not have the second authentication factor, which is usually a temporary code that is generated randomly and is normally valid for 30 seconds.

Ramsomware attacks

How worried should you be about the ransomware that you've been hearing about in the news? This section details everything you need to know about ransomware, including how to protect yourself from a ransomware attack and how to remove it if you become infected.

Cybersecurity is a major problem in today's world, both in the field of the company and on a personal level. Our equipment, portable devices, smart homes and devices connected to the Internet are vulnerable to various attacks. In 2017 alone, over 35,000 million security attacks against PC and 208 million against Android mobile devices were blocked. What was one of the greatest threats to security? The ransomware.

Ransomware is so prevalent today that, quite frankly, it deserves its own chapter.

Chapter 3
The Growing Threat of Ransomware

What is ransomware?

Ransomware is a type of malicious software (also called "malware") designed to hijack computer files and, sometimes, even the entire computer. The malware encrypts your files so they cannot be opened or completely blocks the user's access to the computer, so you cannot see any of your precious videos, photos, accounting files, work documents, etc. Subsequently, the attackers who have sent the malware contact the user to request a ransom and promise to decrypt the files after payment (often required in bitcoins).

Ransomware is not something new. The first known attack occurred in 1989 and spread from one computer to another by means of a diskette. In today's world, where everything is connected in a network, easy access to open source ransomware programs and the great potential of economic benefits have boosted the popularity of this type of malware.

Ransomware attacks consist of a type of malicious software designed to block access to a computer system until a sum of money is paid.

Ransomware is becoming popular and hackers are increasingly recognizing the financial benefits of employing such tactics. The ransomware-based attack occurs when a hacker infects a PC or server, either with malicious software shutting down its system (locker-ransomware) or by custom encryption of important files in its system and demanding a ransom (usually in bitcoins) to change of your systems/files (crypto-ransomware).

Is ransomware a virus?

Most of us know the term "virus" and the IT community mostly uses it to refer to all types of malware. In all actuality, a virus is just one of the many types of malware that exist. Other common types are worms, trojans, spyware and the ransomware. Each type of malware has a specific purpose. The worms replicate and reduce the performance of the computer. Viruses are designed to infect your computer, cause file corruption, and then spread to new hosts. The Trojans are looking for a secret back door to access the equipment and get their personal information. The reasons that lead cybercriminals to create and distribute these types of malware are numerous.

In the case of ransomware, the reason is very clear: the attacker wants money. In general, the purpose is not to damage or destroy the files forever. It is not even about stealing your identity, but about convincing you to pay for the decryption key.

Ransomware on PCs

Anyone can be the target of a ransomware attack. The most talked about ransomware attacks of 2017 and 2018 affected both individuals and companies, including large corporations, hospitals, airports and government agencies.

The personal computer is still the most popular target of ransomware attacks. The hackers exploit known vulnerabilities, especially in the Windows operating system. With that having been said, Apple Macintosh and Linux-based operating systems are not safe from ransomware either.

In May 2017, the WannaCry ransomware quickly spread across the planet and attacked more than 100 million users. It was one of the most highly reported ransomware hacks, and put the fear of ransomware beyond the IT community and into the common household.

WannaCry took advantage of EternalBlue, a known weak point in Windows that was created to assist the NSA. It is an error that allows hackers to execute code remotely using a Windows file and printer sharing request. Two months before the WannaCry attack, Microsoft had released a patch for EternalBlue; Unfortunately, there were many people and companies that did not install the update in time to avoid the attack. The origin of EternalBlue is found in Windows XP, an operating system for which Microsoft no longer offers support, which is why its users were the most affected by WannaCry.

I reference WannaCry very frequently in my speaking engagments on cybersecurity, and the reason is that every hospital, workplace, and home that was compromised was compromised because they did not patch their operating system. It was a completely avoidable tragedy that affected over 300,000 computers worldwide.

Ransomware on mobile devices

Ransomware attacks on mobile devices are increasingly occurring more frequently. Attacks on Android devices increased by 50 percent between 2016 and 2017. Frequently, ransomware is introduced into these devices through an application downloaded from a third-party page. However, we have also seen cases in which the ransomware was hidden within seemingly legitimate applications in the Google Play Store.

The ransomware in Apple products

As mentioned before, Apple fans are not saved either. Previously, Mac users considered themselves less susceptible to malware attacks. However, the growth of market share of Apple products has made malware developers pay more attention. In 2017, two security companies discovered ransomware and spyware programs specially designed to attack Apple users. It is believed that the developers were software engineers specialized in OS X. In addition, the authors of this malware came to make it available, free of charge, on the dark web. The malicious attackers have also accessed the iCloud accounts of Mac users and have used the Find my iPhone service to prevent people from using their computers.

Types of ransomware

Ransomware can take various forms. In all of them, the common denominator is the request for a ransom. In 2017, there were some cases of attacks on institutions with software similar to ransomware, but it did not seem that there was an economic mobile, it is possible that ransomware was used to hide espionage activities or some other type of cyber-attack.

Cryptographic Malware

The most common type of ransomware is cryptographic or encryption: this ransomware encrypts files. You can log in to the computer, but the files cannot be opened. WannaCry is an excellent example of this type of ransomware.

Blocker

The blocking ransomware completely blocks your access to the computer and prevents you from logging on. The Petya ransomware, which emerged in 2016 and returned in 2017 with more sophistication, encrypts the master table of files on the hard drive in order to block the device.

Doxware

Doxware downloads a copy of your confidential files to the attacker's computer, which then threatens to publish them on the Internet if the ransom is not paid. Imagine that someone is threatening to post their most personal photos or videos on a public website where everyone can see them. The Ransoc ransomware used this method.

Scareware

Scareware is a fake software program that claims to have encountered problems in the computer and requests money to fix them. This type of ransomware can flood the screen with windows and alert messages or block the device until it is paid.

One of the factors that have contributed the most to the popularization of ransomware is that it is a type of malware that is easily found on the network and anyone with bad intentions can use it. Avast has observed that about one third of all "new" varieties of ransomware come from an existing open source variety. In addition, hackers are continually updating the code to refine ransomware and improve encryption, so a variety of ransomware can resurface several times, as is the case with Petna.

As the ultimate goal of the attacker is to spread the ransomware on as many computers as possible to get more money, an alternative tactic has appeared to ask for the ransom.

In the case of the Popcorn Time ransomware, the offender asks the victim to infect two other users. If those two users pay the ransom, the first victim can recover their files without having to pay anything.

How are the devices infected?

The most worrying thing about ransomware is that, unlike viruses, it can attack devices without users doing anything. In the case of viruses, the user has to download an infected file or click on an infected link, but the ransomware can infect a vulnerable computer on its own.

Exploit Kits - Malicious attackers develop exploit kits that contain written code designed to take advantage of vulnerabilities such as EternalBlue, described above. This type of ransomware can infect any networked device that has outdated software. One day, we turn on the equipment and oh! All files are blocked.

Social engineering - Other forms of ransomware use proven methods to infect computers. The social engineering (or phishing) refers to the act of persuading someone to download malware from an attachment or a web link. These files usually arrive in an email that appears to come from a reliable source, and the attachment or link resembles an order form, a voucher, an invoice or an important notice. By its extension, the file looks like a PDF or an Excel or Word file, but, in reality, it is a masked executable file. The user downloads it, clicks on it and the debacle begins. (It may not be something instantaneous, some types of ransomware are designed to hide on the computer for a certain period of time, so it is more difficult to find out exactly where they came from).

Malvertising - Malvertising is another method of infection by which the attacker uses an ad network to distribute the malware. The fake ad could appear even on trusted websites. If the user clicks on the ad link, the ransomware is downloaded to their computer.

Silent downloads store malicious files on the computer without any direct action on the part of the user. Some unreliable sites take advantage of browsers and outdated applications to surreptitiously download malware on your computer when you are innocently surfing the Internet. Whichever method the ransomware has reached the computer, when the program is run, it usually works as follows: it starts to modify files (or file structures) so that they can only be re-read or used to restore them to their state original. To protect the communication between the malware and the control equipment (the one used by the offender to manipulate the victim's PC), encryption is used.

When all the files are blocked, a ransom note appears on the screen indicating the amount you must pay to decrypt the files, where or how to transfer the funds and how much time you have to do it. If the deadline is not met, the sum increases. If you try to open any of the encrypted files, an error message appears stating that the file is corrupted, invalid, or missing.

How is ransomware eliminated?

At its core, eliminating and removing the ransomware is not so complicated. If the attacker has used encryption ransomware and the computer can be accessed, you can put it in safe mode and run an antivirus scan to find and remove the malware.

If the ransomware used is the one that blocks access to the computer completely, there are three options: you can reinstall the operating system; run an antivirus program from an external drive or boot disk; or restore the system and restore Windows to a point prior to the ransomware infection.

How are the files recovered?

Unfortunately, removing the ransomware does not mean that suddenly all the encrypted files are accessed. The ease or difficulty of recovering the data depends on the level of encryption. If it's a basic ransomware that uses basic encryption, using one of the many free ransomware decryption tools available on the internet can help. If the computer is infected with a more sophisticated ransomware, such as WannaCry, which uses encryption, it may even be impossible to recover the blocked files.

Some readers may be thinking that the best way to recover the files is to directly pay the ransom. Many people do it, and that's why ransomware has become such a popular form of malware. If the cybercriminals continue to fill their pockets, they will continue to create ransomware.

However, you should never forget this: *there is no guarantee that the attacker will keep his promise to decrypt the files after payment. It is possible that he keeps the money and disappears. It can also happen that, if you see that the victim is willing to pay, increase the amount of the ransom immediately. In addition, the willingness to pay can turn us into targets of another attack in the future.*

It should also be noted that some types of ransomware have such poor coding that, once the files are encrypted, they can no longer be deciphered and are lost forever. This is the case of Petna, for example. So, even if the victim pays, he may not recover the files.

Protection against ransomware: how to prevent a ransomware attack

The best way to deal with a ransomware attack is to prevent it from happening. To do this, follow the following recommendations:

Update the operating system and applications

Yes, we already know that these Windows system update warnings can be a bit annoying, but do not ignore them. (Neither should you ignore the updates of mobile devices or devices connected to the Internet). Many system updates contain security patches, which are essential when it comes to ensuring the security of the devices. If you continue to use an older operating system, such as Windows XP, for which Microsoft no longer supports, you are a victim especially vulnerable to attacks and you should take seriously the issue of upgrading to a newer operating system.

It is also important to update the computer software, especially web browsers and add-ons. Beyond that, I've personally found that many users are mostly unaware of the amount of add-ons on their browsers. It's important to uninstall the add-ons that you are not using because they are each a different vulnerability and security risk.

Back up your files

It is important that you perform periodic system backups on an external storage platform, such as a USB hard drive, a NAS drive, or cloud storage. At a minimum, you should make a backup copy of the most important and valuable files so that they are protected against malware and hard drive failures. Nowadays, storage costs very little and there are numerous options, both USB type and NAS type. There are also many free cloud storage systems, such as Dropbox, Google

Drive, MEGA and OneDrive. Because of the plethora of backup storage options that are available on the market today, there is absolutely no excuse to not backup your data.

Install antivirus software

Although cyberattacks are usually targeted at businesses, viruses occur at an extremely high frequency and are much more common. Although a virus does not typically encrypt data, they can steal it and infect your computer, decreasing productivity. Most modern anti-virus software can often block the attack of 99% of known viruses. Anti-virus companies work together to identify new threats and viruses, and patch them accordingly. It can also protect you against spyware designed to spy on your company's actions and save your data. It also protects you from unwanted spam, which no one wants to deal with. Find good antivirus software that scans and updates daily to keep your computers and data secure.

Use of firewall

While antivirus software can usually detect a virus and get rid of it, a firewall prevents it from reaching your computer in the first place. A firewall can be thought of as a filter that sits between your computer and the Internet. When you browse the Web, you constantly send and receive packets of information. A firewall filters out these packets and acts as a shield to anyone that could be harmful. However, it is important to note that there is no firewall that is perfect. If a virus can get through, a firewall cannot remove it. If a lock can be made by man, it can be broken by man.

Stay alert to social engineering manipulation techniques

It goes without saying that you never have to open files or click on links that come from unknown sources. If you receive an email with a dubious attachment, delete it without even opening it. If you know the sender of the email, you can talk directly to them and ask them if the attached file is legitimate. Remember to also be aware of messages that invite you to click on links that lead to malicious websites; They could be in an email, a text message or even on social networks. When entering personal data, make sure 100% that the page has HTTPS protocol enabled. And how do you know? Look for the green padlock symbol in the browser: a visual indication that ensures the page is secure.

Chapter 4
Why Criminals Want Data

Why cyber criminals attack companies

The latest report published by the firm Techco Security analyzes the keys and motivations of cybercriminals in their attacks. Money, but also revenge or ideological issues are just some of them.

It is not necessary to be a candidate for the presidency of the United States so that a group of cybercriminals try to interfere in our interests and tilt the electoral process to one side or the other. What does this mean? Well, anonymous as we are or as irrelevant that we believe our personal data is for others, we are all potential victims of a cyber-attack.

Small to midsized busineses are especially vulnerable in this regard. A few months ago, the National Cybersecurity Institute (INCIBE) predicted that in 2016 it would manage around 100,000 digital aggressions in some countries of the world against various objectives, although more than two thirds would be aimed at small and medium-sized companies.

The National Intelligence Center (CNI) is a bit more conservative and estimates that Spanish companies will close 2016 with more than 25,000 cyber-attacks, with an increase of 64% in the small and medium-sized companies' segment and 44% in large companies, if we take as reference 2014.

The information and data handled by companies makes them very sweet targets. SMEs because of their vulnerability and large corporations because of the enormous amount of credentials they can store.

The recent DDoS attack that knocked down a good part of the Internet just a few weeks ago, taking ahead of mastodons like Twitter or Spotify, is a good example of this. But it also infected common user devices connected to the Internet of Things.

And is that there are many and diverse motivations that can lead these criminals to perform these cyber-attacks. The money is the most obvious and the one that is often behind many of them: the ransomware, for example, gives them access to the user's credentials and they take control of their services (usually banking) remotely, being able to extract money when they please or demanding a ransom for the stolen information.

Another way to profit economically is by selling to third parties the access data and passwords that they steal, and also the images they obtain by infecting the camera of the user's devices.

But there are many more reasons that can be hidden behind a cyber-attack: ideological, personal, strategic, political or revenge. There are organizations that offer their services to anyone who wants to harm through the network but does not know how.

Chapter 5
How to Protect your Data

Typical cyber security measures companies use to protect themselves

Despite huge challenges around data recovery, SMEs do not always have the means to surround themselves with a specialized support function in this area and favor other investments. Yet this same study by IPSOS has shown that the budget that should be spent on IT protection is nothing, compared to what it costs, in repair, a violation of a company's computer system ... Computer protection would constitute therefore a profitable investment, as well as other development investments within the company.

At a time when widespread cyberattacks are regularly in the media to the point of paralyzing large companies like Renault, we thought that a reminder of some basic rules would not be luxury!

Here are some of the ways through which companies protect themselves against cyber-security attack:

Conformity on security measures

If the establishment of security measures on certain internet sites is too complicated for users, many of them will desist from protecting their data and key information. "There must be continuous audits of the security systems of the usual sites used by the employees of the company to ensure that they comply with the protection standards necessary to protect information and internal network systems," they underline.

Software update

Updates of software and software, in addition to incorporating improvements, also tend to add more advanced protectors against viruses, although this task (update) does not fall directly on the employee. The software update has to be a continuous responsibility of the IT department. If employees browse their browser with outdated or outdated anti-malware solutions, cybercriminals could take advantage of possible attacks as a point of entry into the network.

Regularly updating the operating system and the software installed on all the computers used within the company, and paying special attention to updates to the web browser is a crucial practice to make sure all employees within a company are using. Sometimes, operating systems have flaws, which can be exploited by computer criminals. Updates often appear that solve these faults. Being up to date with the updates, as well as applying the security patches recommended by the manufacturers, has been of immense help to companies in preventing the possible intrusion of hackers and the appearance of new viruses.

Cybersecurity rules for those who want to protect their business

Small companies and business owners, as well as any Internet users, should not lose their vigilance against cyber threats today. Anyone can be a victim of hacker attacks.

The mistake of many professionals unexperienced in cyber hygiene is the absolute certainty that their business is not interesting for cyber-criminals. However, it is precisely this neglect and the use of outdated security tools by companies without the use of current technologies and security techniques are often sufficient arguments for hackers to select such companies as a victim and decide to launch an attack. In addition, a small organization can be chosen as a springboard to attack its partner company using weak links in the supply chain of goods or services.

Here are some tips on how to best approach security if you have a small business.

Do not rely on antivirus, but make sure you are using one

It's no secret that traditional antivirus solutions alone are not able to cope with most modern threats. Back in 2014, the company Norton Antivirus loudly said: " Antivirus is dead." Norton admitted that the traditional antivirus detected only 45% of all attacks. Even at the 2014 standards level, this figure does not look optimistic. Today, according to the most loyal estimates, they detect from 20 to 40% of attacks.

Since its introduction in 1987, antiviruses have used binary signa-tures (hashes) to identify malicious files. Today, signatures have lost their effectiveness, as modern attacks are constantly changing and evolving, they have learned to bypass detection in this way. Of course, antiviruses also do not stand still - they have functions of heuristic analysis and detection of threats for which there are no corresponding signatures in the database, but there are similar ones. However, this approach has a very high false positive rate. In addition, after instal-lation, such an antivirus significantly loads the system, taking up too much space on the hard disk and using additional processor power.

Do not open the door to hackers

Companies that want to create a truly effective protection system need to take a number of steps. First of all, you need to understand exactly how malware can penetrate your network. Most malware enters the system through exploits, programming errors, or vulner-abilities. Preventing the use of exploits will help you defend against unknown threats.

First of all, it is necessary to teach your colleagues and employees never to open attachments and not to click on links in letters if they come from a source in which you cannot be 100% sure.

Many seemingly safe organizations very often turn out to be malware guides. The best defense is to not initially create a "door" for a hacker to your system. These rules have been repeated many times already, but we still register a huge number of hacks precisely because of the human factor. The so-called social engineering is one of the most effective tools of cybercriminals, because, as you know, the weakest link in computing systems is the human being.

What can be done?

It requires solutions that analyze the behavior of files and traffic. They must be able to prevent attacks and at the same time have a means of detection for those cases where the attackers still entered the system through any loopholes. Such protection is needed everywhere - on end and mobile devices, in data centers, the cloud and even on IoT devices. This is a class of solutions called sandboxes or threat emulators. They track files and programs with suspicious behavior, put them in a sandbox test environment, launch and watch how they will behave in an isolated environment to avoid negative impact on work in the work network. If everything is in order, and no malicious activity is detected, the file enters the company's computer system.

Think over protection strategy

For a business of any size, the same rules apply: first you need to determine which data is most important for the owner, and then choose solutions to protect them and reduce the risk of loss. Until recently, this required a disproportionately large investment in security. Today, start-up companies have the same opportunities as major players, for reasonable money.

First, consider the cloud model. It gives organizations the ability to quickly deploy and manage security systems with cloud service providers, with little or no up-front investment and predictable monthly costs. In addition, this way you can deploy advanced integrated services: from antivirus and firewalls to web applications and social network management tools. This allows companies to focus on the challenges of business and development, leaving the protection of the network to professionals.

Secondly, medium and small businesses today have access to comprehensive integrated protection capabilities that only large enterprises could use before (working in virtual private networks, intrusion prevention, antispam, application control and URL filtering). Their cost starts from a few hundred dollars. This allows many companies to fit advanced security capabilities into even the most limited IT budget.

The main thing - an integrated approach to security. It is necessary to include the above-mentioned antiviruses, firewalls, and systems to prevent DDoS attacks and antibot solutions.

Pay special attention to mobile devices.

Today, any business is increasingly moving towards mobility. Startups often store corporate data on laptops and smartphones or in public cloud storages, which can be accessed from any gadget. And this is the weakest point in terms of business information security.

The most promising approach to mobile protection is the isolation inside the mobile device of an isolated container for working with and storing corporate data.

Thus, with your personal information in the smartphone, the user can do anything except hacking the device. To resolve any work issues, you need to switch to a protected container and enter an additional pin code. Only then will access to corporate data and resources. Through the established VPN tunnel, the user will be able to access corporate mail, calendar, address book and other applications. Then corporate data will be completely isolated from personal. Files, mail - all this is securely protected and managed centrally as part of corporate security policy.

Many still believe that hackers are scary tales that IT security experts scare their management. But the statistics cannot be fooled. According to annual survey on cyber security, valuable data is sent out of an organization every 32 minutes, and every four seconds one unknown malicious program is downloaded to the company's network, which is known every 81 seconds. And while this attitude will dominate, these numbers will grow.

Part 2
The Internet of Things

The world right now is faced with an astronomical increase in digital technology. Every aspect of our lives is being affected by one form of digital technology, and communication. The way it stands now, the rapid technological changes have paved the way for different aspects of our lives to have a sort of connection with the Internet.

Billions of people in the world today are connected to the Internet in one form or the other, and the number of devices connected to the Internet is well on its way to exceeding billions in the near future. The Internet of Things provides a profound change in the digital world, and its effects have their footprints in individual interactions as well as various businesses.

IoT (Internet of Things) is a way of describing the global connection of devices, and objects interacting with the physical environment, people, and each other. IoT is hard to define, because its definition and scope can vary depending on which expert you speak to. In a layman's term, it can loosely be defined as the connection of every device to the Internet. In a more technical outlook, IoT can be described as the interaction of physical objects and the Internet via the aid of systems and sensors, in order to create tangible results, and meaningful convenience for the end-user community. The IoT establishes an avenue for various kinds of services and interactions that range from as little as smartphone integration to as large as smart city services.

In just a matter of time, sensors and visualization tools will be birthed by the IoT, and these tools and much more will be made available to people - at any time, and anywhere, and on any device on both an individual, business, cooperate or even community level. There is excellent potential to how the IoT can continue to affect our lives, and the unlimited capabilities are what makes it a prospering and a growing venture.

The change that IoT is implementing on the world is not the fact that objects are interacting with one another, but the fact that people are relying more and more on it through the various objects in their possession. It is the IoT that provides the medium of connection for people, and because in this day and age, human interactions and communication now rely on a form of machine or object, there is the ever-growing concern of cyber threats and problems.

IoT devices are heavily reliant on cloud computing, different forms of applications, as well as smart devices with inbuilt sensors to function. This dependency on cloud computing for its operations coupled with the fact that at present, there is no viable integrated platform yet to house the connected technology, means that Cybersecurity has to improve drastically. With the number of connected devices used for interactions increasing on a daily basis, there is now an even more significant challenge in data safety, protection, and privacy.

With all of this having being said, Cybersecurity and the IoT must go hand in hand. For the IoT to fully actualize its potential, and be the face of the future, then Cybersecurity most play a prominent role in. The IoT possess great opportunities and at the same time challenges that need rapt attention most especially from the Security side of things.

Chapter 6
Defining the Internet
of Things

What is the Internet of Things?

A new level of technological advances that makes wireless communication possible via a dynamic set of connected devices with the view of improving how we live and work the Internet of Things: the linking of information through networks comprising of technologies like sensors placed within physical objects such as home automation systems, electronic tags, and so on. Just like how the Internet connects the seven billion inhabitants of the world, so is the IoT expected to offer such connection for networks, devices, and IT systems.

When it started, the Internet was a utility only those with computers could access, but with the increase in technology, and worldwide development, the last few years has since it allowed it to develop into something truly astounding. In the modern world today, there are different sensors in the form of mobile devices, home appliances, and even vehicles to be connected in one way to the web. Internet gadgets are a common theme in the work environment and home environment. An example of this would be Google home and other AI-enabled devices. You see, all these devices all form part of what is considered the Internet of Things trend, and in the nearest future, it is expected that everything around us will have a form of Internet function, thereby making virtually every task done at work or at home more efficiently.

As stated before, having one universal definition of the Internet of Things isn't an easy proposition as various persons have their point of view as regards the subject matter. Some experts focus on the potential revenues that will be amassed in trillions when defining it regarding market size, while others place emphasis on the number of potential sensors like smartphones, tablets and other devices that could rise up to several billion in the coming years. These varying points of focus, can morph what their definition of IoT is.

The Internet of Things at its core is the network of physical objects that contain embedded technologies to communicate, sense, and interact within themselves or the external environment. In other words, it is simply connecting all things in the world to the Internet. IoT is the future of the Internet in which systems and objects are designed with sensors, and computing prowess, with the intention of having these objects communicate effortlessly with each other. Although the initial concept of IoT was to place emphasis on communications involving Machine to Machine, the bigger picture is to place emphasis on communications involving people directly or indirectly.

With each passing day, there is an increase in networking capabilities, objects, machines, and devices in the office and home environment.

This is seen in office equipment, vehicles, home devices, wearable devices, and urban infrastructures. In a way, this creates a whole new level of opportunities for individuals and businesses alike.

IoT thrives on sensor-based technologies, such that the sensor identifies changes in location and position, and then transmit the information in the form of data to a server or device, which in turn analyze the information and data, in order to produce the needed information for the end-user. On the business side of things, sensors act as means to gather data, with cloud computing serving as the platform for the storing, and analyzing of the generated data, and with Big Data Analytics providing a means of turning that data into useful insights, information and knowledge.

In employing IoT for business practices, different business will have diverse applications for IoT. From manufacturing to core operations, and even services, each business model will have its own way of making use of IoT. Let's take a retail store as an example and see the benefit IoT can provide in the future. A customer may walk into a boutique, and the measuring sensors will quickly take a measurement of his/her body size, with the generated data sent through the cloud on available stock pertaining to the initial measurements taken, and then, the inventory will quickly be replenished based on the measurement provided. This is just one of the ways IoT can be utilized. There are also other ventures that the IoT comes into play in such as mobile payments and other sensors.

Chapter 7
How the Internet of Things Works

How IoT works

When something is connected to the Internet, it means that it can either send or receive information, or do both simultaneously. A typical example of this is your handheld device like your smartphones. You can listen to any song in the world or watch any video in the world with it. This happens not because your phone has all the songs and videos in it, but because these files are stored up somewhere. Now, your phone can ask for that video by sending an information request and then receive the information to enable it to play the video or song. In a way, your smartphone helps you connect to storage so you can have access to your needed information.

On an individualistic scale, there are several science fictions that depict smart homes in which appliances seem to have a mind of their own, and start to function automatically. As soon as the alarm sounds, the coffee pot kicks in and starts to brew. Lights come to life as you walk past each section of the home, and the car just drives you to work on its own while taking the route of least congestion. All these may seem science fictional, but they are coming into being reality (or are very close for some) because of the Internet of Things.

We've already established that IoT consists of all the web-enabled devices that collect, send and act on data they obtain from their environments with the aid of embedded sensors, and processors. These devices sometimes referred to as connected devices are used for Human to Machine interactions, Machine to Machine interactions and Human to Human interactions. The Internet of Things makes each of these interactions and connections much easier by offering a coordinated platform for their utilization. It, therefore, means people can interact with gadgets, and gadgets can interact with themselves to provide business and individual solutions.

Physical objects and devices come with built-in sensors that are connected to one of the several Internet of Things platforms. These platforms integrate data from various devices and carry the necessary analytics to provide the most valuable information needed by the end user. These platforms can locate the useful information that is required, and ignore the useless information. With such useful information, patterns can be detected, recommendations can be made, and even problems can be averted before they occur.

Similar to the way the Internet has changed the way people communicate, work, and interact with one another by connecting everyone via the Internet itself, IoT aims to take the connectivity to a whole stage by aiding the connection of multiple devices at a single time to the Internet and in that way, facilitate humans to machine, and machine to machine communication. As a field, the IoT is a very dynamic field, with various uses and potential in not just individual lives, but also in business applications spanning from home automation, retail, vehicle automation, agriculture, Healthcare and lots more.

To know better how IoT works, first, let's take a look at the four fundamental components of IoT system.

- Devices/Sensors

- Connectivity/Connection

- Data Processing

- User interface

- Device/Sensors

Without any sensor or device, there really isn't any IoT as this is where it starts from. First, the sensors collect the necessary data from the surrounding environment. This data could range from different levels of complexities from as simple as a temperature reading to more complex video transmission.

Different sensors can be found in various devices, and in some cases, certain devices have multiple sensors functioning together. Like take a phone for instance, on its own, the phone doesn't sense things, but it has several sensors built in, like a camera, GPS, and lots more. These sensors help to pick and collect the necessary data from the environment.

Connection/Connectivity

After the collection of the data, the next point of action is to send the data to a cloud for storage, analysis, and feedback, but before the data and info can get to the cloud, it needs a transporting medium, and hence the need for connections and connectivity.

The sensor/devices are connected to the cloud infrastructure by different kinds of connectivity transports, like Wi-Fi, Cellular network, Wide Area Networks (WAN), Satellite network, Bluetooth and lots more.

Depending on the nature of connection utilized, expect different specifications to the bandwidth, and range. The best connectivity option is essential to the IoT system.

Data processing

What good is any data if it cannot be processed into a tangible output or information? The penultimate component of IoT is data processing. As soon as the data is gathered and sent to the cloud, the software carries out the processing on the acquired data.

This can be in the form of something simple like checking to see that the temperature values on an Air conditioning unit are within the desired range. It can be as complicated as trying to run facial recognition through computer vision. All this processed data would be useless if there is no user at the end of it, and this leads to the last component, user-interface.

User-interface

Via notifications, alarm systems, or trigger systems, the needed information is made available to the end-user. In a way, the user can also gain insight into their IoT system and make the necessary adjustments or actions with respect to the information placed before it. Sometimes, machine to machine interaction is needed to process the information, depending on the type of actions, and predefined rules choosing. Human interaction might not be needed as the machine/devices can make the necessary changes with the processed data.

These four components help explain how IoT works both in an individual setting, as well as in a business setting. A typical business example will be:

For example, a car manufacturing business might want to know which optional components (leather seats or alloy wheels, for example) are the most popular. Using the Internet of Things technology, they can:

- Use sensors to detect which areas in a showroom are the most popular, and where customers linger longest;

- Drill down into the available sales data to identify which components are selling fastest;

- Automatically align sales data with supply, so that favorite items don't go out of stock.

The information picked up by connected devices enables the business to make smart decisions about which components to stock up on, based on real-time information, which helps them to save time and money.

With the insight provided by advanced analytics comes the power to make processes more efficient. Smart objects and systems mean you can automate specific tasks, particularly when these are repetitive, mundane, time-consuming or even dangerous. Let's look at some examples to see what this looks like in real life. Another example (futuristic example) of the IoT in action, can be seen in the retail and merchandising sector, for example; if a new customer enters a shoe shop, his or her shoe size could be measured by the measurement sensors; data could be sent over the cloud about the availability of stock; the inventory could then be replenished based on real-time analytics and forecasted trends

Chapter 8
Practical Uses for the Internet of Things

Some practical uses of the internet of things we see today

The Internet of Things promises to bring immense value to our lives both individually and in a business environment, and it is already achieving such great feats with outstanding applications. Through the connection of all things in the world, there is an endless possibility to what can be achieved. The emergence of IoT has seen its application in different practical aspects of our daily lives, from home down to business, and also other vital sectors of the environment. Let's take a deeper dive into some of the most popular use cases for IoT.

Smart home application

Imagine the ability to switch on the air conditioning before reaching home. Imagine that you could switch off lights even after you have left home. Or you could unlock the doors to friends for temporary access even when you are not at home. Don't be surprised - with IoT taking shape companies are building products to make your life simpler and more convenient than it ever has been before.

Smart Home has become the revolutionary ladder of success in the residential spaces, and it is predicted that smart homes will become as common as smartphones within the next few decades.

The cost of owning a house is the most significant expense in many people's lives. Smart Home products are promised to save time, energy and money. With Smart home companies like Nest, Ecobee, Ring, and August, to name a few, will become household brands and are planning to deliver a never seen before experience.

It is impossible to ignore the impact that IoT technologies have had on our homes. Smart appliances, lighting, security, and environmental controls make our life more comfortable and more convenient. Nest is among the leaders in this sphere. With some smart devices, including Nest Thermostat, indoor cameras, and alarms, on the go helps for better home management.

The thermostat learns about your preferences and automatically adjusts the temperature. In addition to a comfortable environment at home, it will help you save on heating and use your energy more efficiently. Nest Indoor and Outdoor Cameras together with smoke and CO alarms make your home a safer place.

The best part about Nest smart home products is the fact that you can monitor and manage all of these devices with your smartphone using a dedicated app.

Wearables

Wearables have experienced an explosive demand in markets all over the world. Companies like Google, Samsung, and Amazon have invested heavily in building such devices.

Wearable devices are installed with sensors and software which collect data and information about the users. This data is later pre-processed to extract essential insights about the user.

These devices broadly cover fitness, health and entertainment requirements. The pre-requisite from the internet of things technology for wearable applications is to be highly energy efficient or ultralow power and small sized.

Such wearable devices monitor heart rate, caloric intake, sleep, track activity, and many other metrics to help us stay healthy. In some cases, such wearables can communicate with third-party apps and share information about the user's chronic conditions with a health-care provider.

In addition to the personal use of health wearables, there are some advanced smart appliances, including scales, thermometers, blood pressure monitors, and even hair brushes

Connected Cars

The automotive digital technology has focused on optimizing vehicles internal functions. But now, this attention is growing towards enhancing the in-car experience.

A connected car is a vehicle which can optimize its own operation, maintenance as well as the comfort of passengers using onboard sensors and internet connectivity.

Most large automakers, as well as some brave startups, are working on connected car solutions. Major brands like Tesla, BMW, Apple, Google are working on bringing the next revolution in automobiles.

There are also mobile applications connects to a connected device, which allows you to control such functions of your car as opening/closing the doors, engine metrics, the alarm system, detecting the car's location and routes, etc.

While connected or even self-driven cars have already become a reality, automotive IoT use cases are actively expanding to other types of ground transport, including railway transport.

Smart Cities

A smart city is another powerful application of IoT generating curiosity among the world's population. Smart surveillance, automated transportation, more intelligent energy management systems, water distribution, urban security, and environmental monitoring all are examples of the internet of things applications for smart cities.

IoT will solve significant problems faced by the people living in cities like pollution, traffic congestion and a shortage of energy supplies, etc. Products like cellular communication enabled Smart Belly trash will send alerts to municipal services when a bin needs to be emptied.

By installing sensors and using web applications, citizens can find free available parking slots across the city. Also, the sensors can detect meter tampering issues, general malfunctions, and any installation issues in the electricity system.

IoT in agriculture

With the continuous increase in the world's population, the demand for food supply is enormously raised. Governments are helping farmers to use advanced techniques and research to increase food production. Smart farming is one of the fastest growing fields in IoT. Smart farming is often overlooked when it comes to business cases for IoT solutions. However, there are many innovative products on the market geared toward forward-thinking farmers

Farmers are using meaningful insights from the data to yield a better return on investment. Sensing for soil moisture and nutrients, controlling water usage for plant growth and determining custom fertilizer are some simple uses of IoT. Some of them use a distributed network of smart sensors to monitor various natural conditions, such as humidity, air temperature, and soil quality. Others are used to automate irrigation systems.

For outdoor agriculture, an example could be sensing soil moisture and taking weather into account so that smart irrigation systems only water crops when needed, reducing the amount of water usage.

For indoor agriculture, IoT allows monitoring and management of micro-climate conditions (humidity, temperature, light, etc.) to maximize production.

Using IoT applications to gather data about the health and wellbeing of the cattle, ranchers knowing early about the sick animal can pull out and help prevent a large number of sick cows. Livestock monitoring is about animal husbandry and cost saving.

Smart Retail

The potential of IoT in the retail sector is enormous. IoT provides an opportunity for retailers to connect with customers to enhance the in-store experience.

Smartphones will be the way for retailers to remain connected with their consumers even out of the store. Interacting through

Smartphones and using Beacon technology can help retailers serve their consumers better. They can also track consumers path through a store and improve store layout and place premium products in high traffic areas.

By placing RFID or NFC tags on individual products, the exact location of single items in a large warehouse can be shared, thus saving search time and lowering labor costs.

Another example is in a retail setting. By knowing precisely what's in stock and what isn't, the store can order new products only when needed. This reduces the cost of keeping extra inventory in the back. Also, smart inventory management eliminates the need to manually check what's on the shelves, reducing labor costs.

Energy Engagement

Power grids of the future will be not only smart enough but also highly reliable. Smart grid concept is becoming very popular all over the world.

The basic idea behind the smart grids is to collect data in an automated fashion and analyze the behavior of consumers and suppliers for improving efficiency as well as the economics of electricity use.

Smart Grids will also be able to detect sources of power outages more quickly and at individual household levels like nearby solar panel, making possible distributed energy system.

People and organizations can achieve significant decreases in their energy usage with IoT. Sensors monitor things like lighting, temperature, energy usage, etc. and that data is processed by intelligent algorithms to micromanage activities in real-time.

On an individual level, things like Smart Thermostats can automatically turn off heating/cooling when no one's home to save energy.

IoT in Healthcare

Connected healthcare yet remains the sleeping giant of the Internet of Things applications. The concept of a connected healthcare system and smart medical devices bears enormous potential not just for companies, but also for the well-being of people in general.

Research shows IoT in healthcare will be massive in the coming years. IoT in healthcare is aimed at empowering people to live healthier lives by wearing connected devices.

The collected data will help in the personalized analysis of an individual's health and provide tailor-made strategies to combat illness. The video below explains how IoT can revolutionize treatment and medical help.

The Internet of Things enables heightened surveillance, monitoring, and detection, which all combine to improve health and increase safety.

Chapter 9
Cybersecurity and IoT

What the internet of things means for cybersecurity

A defining element of the Internet of Things is that objects are not inherently smart, and that means they are equipped with sensors and processing power, but also, they are connected, and that means they can share the information they generate. What separates the IoT from the traditional Internet is the exclusion of people. The Internet is powered by individuals constantly inputting data in the form of search terms, uploading photos, e-retail browsing, filling an online form, or looking up a friend's Facebook page. Based upon the answers generated, they make decisions about how to act, whether to visit the site, share the page or buy the toaster.

With the IoT, the role of humans reduces, to the point that in many cases they are not part of the equation. The way it now works,

Machines input, communicate, analyze, and act upon the information. Using sensor detection, machines can create information about individuals' behavior, analyze it, and take action—ideally in the form of streamlined, tailored products and services or, in the case of businesses, greater efficiencies. This newfound capability is why the IoT enables enterprises and individuals alike to create value in new ways, at a faster velocity than we've ever seen

There is a dark side, however, is that as data are created and transmitted, this in turn now represents a new opportunity for that information to be compromised. More data, and specifically more sensitive data, available across a broad network means the risks are higher and that data breaches could pose significant dangers to individuals and enterprises alike. Thanks to the IoT, data security risks will very likely go beyond embarrassing privacy leaks too, potentially, the hacking of significant public systems.

While the IoT is entering daily life more and more, security risks about IoT are growing and are changing rapidly. In today's world of hands-on technology and not enough security awareness on the part of users, cyber-attacks are now a common occurrence

Cybercriminals are working on new techniques for getting through the security of established organizations, accessing everything from IP to individual customer information. They are doing this to cause damage, disrupt sensitive data and steal intellectual property.

Every day, their attacks become more sophisticated and harder to defeat. Because of this ongoing development, we cannot tell exactly what kind of threats will emerge next year, in five years' time, or in 10 years' time; we can only say that these threats will be even more dangerous than those of today. We can also be sure that as old sources of this threat fade, new sources will emerge to take their place. It is because of this uncertainty that cybersecurity and IoT are intertwined.

Effective cybersecurity is increasingly complex to deliver. The traditional organizational perimeter is eroding, and existing security defenses are coming under increasing pressure. Point solutions, in particular, antivirus software, intrusion detection and prevention, patching, and encryption remain a crucial control for combatting today's known attacks; however, they become less effective over time as hackers find new ways to circumvent controls

As we continue to become a more connected society, the Internet of Things (IoT) often goes overlooked. Everything from your refrigerator to your alarm clock is connected to the Internet. And it's made our lives easier in many ways. But few people stop to consider how IoT connectedness makes us vulnerable to cyber threats. Internet of Things is a shared ecosystem of interconnected devices, that can talk to each other and share information, without human intervention, to provide insights and improve system's efficiency. With 1.2 billion IoT devices in 2018 and expected growth to 30 billion by 2021, shows the significance of IoT technology. But it is important to keep in mind that with this unprecedented development, comes the risk of security threats. Cybercrime has become a significant issue for IoT devices, due to the vulnerabilities in a shared network, and unavailability of a global standard for such devices.

Cybercrime refers to the use of a computer or network as a tool to commit an offense or illegal activity. Cybersecurity deals with the practices and technologies that are used to prevent such unauthorized access or attacks. The Internet of Things implements a centralized system, where data from all objects and sensors are accumulated in a central server, to provide analytical feedback, to the corresponding system. Due to this, the central server becomes the exposed point of access. Vulnerability in any child node (sensors/objects) can give unauthorized access to the hacker, who can then use it to disable the system or steal private information.

Threats and risks come in these forms:

1. Counterfeiting

Counterfeiting refers to illegal manufacturing and distribution of an original product, to mislead the recipient into believing that they are getting the real product. Counterfeiting in IoT happens by replacement of smart things, cloning by untrusted parties or firmware replacement attacks. This allows the third party to gather personal data, or sniff into the system network, to gain unauthorized access. With a total amount of counterfeit products reaching 1.2 Trillion USD, it's one of the most common forms of crime in society.

2. Denial of service (Botnet)

Denial of Service is a type of cyber-attack, in which a source (DoS) or multiple sources (DDoS) attacks the system, to deny or destruct the use of services, provided by the system. In IoT, it is achieved with the help of Botnets or Thingbots, where many devices are programmed to request the same service simultaneously. Botnets or Thingbots are a network of systems, controlled by botnet operators via Command-and-Control-Servers (C&C Server), to take control of a system and distribute malware through it. These bots are connected via the internet and can transfer data automatically through it. The main aim of botnets is to either crash the target system or make it inaccessible.

3. Eavesdropping (Man-in-the-middle)

In Eavesdropping, a third party utilizing software 'listens' to the interactions between two or more interconnected devices, due to an insecure communication channel. One example of the active eavesdropping mechanism in the IoT industry is the Man-in-the-Middle attack. The Man-in-the-Middle attack in a concept, in which the hacker attempts to disrupt or breach communication between two systems. It intercepts and transmits data, impersonating as another system secretly so that the actual devices wouldn't realize, they have been compromised. This has a hazardous impact on IoT since all the devices are interconnected, so the threat levels are high if any one of the networks is compromised. For example, if a smart door is made to believe it is interacting with a real owner it can open the door of your house, leading to the loss of personal belongings.

4. Buffer overflow

Buffer overflow is a type of cyber-attack, in which a program tries to write more data to buffer (temporary store) than it can hold, leading to crash. It is the most known vulnerability of any system but still exists in today's world. Buffer overflow attack happens in IoT devices, due to the following reasons:

- Memory: IoT devices are built to be energy efficient, hence small memory buffer, which can be easily overflowed.

- Language: Most IoT devices are made on C and C++ language, which doesn't have a garbage collector, leading to an increase in the risk of buffer overflow.

- Commonality: Businesses tend to buy inexpensive programs for their IoT devices, which shares a common code base, making it more vulnerable to cyber-attacks, if any weak spot is found on the standard code.

5. Malicious modification

A malicious modification is a type of attack in which the software code or hardware of IoT devices are altered to inflict damage to the system. It happens after the devices are produced, and before it is installed and used, or when any hacker rewrites a piece of code to gain access to or to disrupt the functionality. Such alterations can lead to abnormality, or total failure of the system or can be used to steal valuable data from the target.

6. Phishing

In Phishing, a hacker tries to obtain your credentials and use it to gain access and then can commit identity fraud, sell your information on the dark web, or ransom accounts. The most common technique is social engineering hacks, in which a hacker sends a link to the user, usually through email promising various offers, and makes you divulge your information, or lets you visit a fake site with a striking resemblance to the original one, in order to gain access to your credentials. Smart devices usually use SSH or SMTP, which can be rigged to send malicious emails, with the help of credentials obtained through phishing.

7. Supply Chain attack

Supply chain attack or value-chain or third-party attack, is a type of cyber-attack, in which a third party infiltrates your system with access, via outside partner or provider. IoT being a shared ecosystem has led to more suppliers and provider having access to the sensitive data, making it more vulnerable to such attacks. IoT devices regularly send diagnostics back to the suppliers for predictive maintenance, but it can also act as a back channel to receive sensitive data from those devices. Hackers focus on weaker networks to gain access, by manipulating devices or hardware. These devices then act as a backdoor for the hackers, through which, they can add malware to the system

Each of these threats can be categorized into the following three forms.

External threats

An external threat is colloquially known as hacking. Because everyday items are now connected to the Internet, they can be hacked just like a computer. This might not seem like a major concern at first. After all, there's not much data a hacker could get from your microwave, right? But the fears deepen when you consider how IoT items that contain cameras or microphones may be compromised.

Another thing to consider is how an external threat can have an impact on a mass scale. What would happen to society if everyone had their alarm clocks hacked and shut off? We didn't need to worry about these types of invisible robberies during the analog age, but we do need to consider these potential problems now. You can take measures to protect your IoT devices. Simple things like a web application firewall, adjusting your settings, and knowing when to take a device offline can make a big difference in your cybersecurity.

Internal threats

If your IoT devices are in the workplace, you can have issues that are different than external hackers. You may have people internally who want to rig the system. Say there's a room with private information that's locked and has restricted access. If your employees are using key card access to get into that room, a savvy employee can manipulate the ID process. But there are also internal threats that are not malicious. Employees with access may unwittingly give information to those who don't have privileges by making a simple technology error. It's vital that everyone in your office who is interacting with IoT devices is adequately trained and understands the impact of their actions. Things like downloading dangerous files can be easily avoided with the proper education.

Disgruntled employees

An employee who is disenfranchised by the workplace can cause severe damage. While you want to know how to manage your IoT from a technology standpoint best, you also need to be in tune with your managers and human data. Employees who want to do the company harm may need counseling or another form of intervention. If a disgruntled employee is a flight risk or if you plan to terminate the employee soon, you need a way to manage their permissions and access quickly. But you can also use IoT to alert you to a disgruntled employee sooner than a real-life manager may notice. Using analytics, you can have certain behaviors flagged. An example of a malicious behavior is if an employee is downloading sensitive company data to their personal computer during non-working hours.

Challenges faced by the Internet of Things in the field of Cyber Security

With the increase of Cybersecurity threats in the IoT field, there is an urgent need to place proper security paradigm in place. However, there are still a few challenges, which are needed to be addressed, before it can be done.

1. Massive Quantities of Exposed IoT Devices

With the exponential growth of IoT technology, there are an enormous number of IoT devices which are resources deficient, and hence vulnerable to all kind of cyber-attacks. These IoT devices have limited capability to run encryption or access control algorithms, due to which DDoS attacks, eavesdropping, or tampering becomes easier.

These attacks can cause large-scale security breaches and a considerable amount of loss.

2. Data Privacy and Security

IoT works by processing sensor data, and more the data, the accurate the analytics. With more IoT devices created every day, it has become difficult to transmit all data to the central server for storage and processing. Edge computing brings centralization to IOT, where all localized data is stored and processed in the client side itself before it is sent to the server. This way, the organization has much more control over the data, but it also raises many security threats. The data stored in edge devices are more susceptible to physical tampering, or DDoS attacks through multiple layers like the perception layer, transport layer, and application layer.

3. Edge communication in IoT Devices and offloading

IoT devices usually have smaller memory and processing power, due to its energy efficient build. These lead to the offloading of tasks to another system with more resources, other IoT devices for processing. These transactions often speed up the processing time but bring in additional security threats. Risk of eavesdropping in wireless communication, cross-platform code migration and dynamic scheduling of offloaded task are few of the challenging tasks for such systems. The edge cloud also needs to keep track of the interaction between those devices, to provide adequate resources to the system.

4. Trust and Trustworthiness

IoT devices, especially edge devices communicate with each other all the time, to share data. These communications are more prone to malicious attacks. The system needs to find those hijacked devices and networks and fix them. Since the primary authentication mechanism is not enough for the security, most of the system uses human-centered digital signature certificates. The issue with such certificates is triggering of recertification, which is time-consuming and expensive. Automated certifications still have a long way to go. Visible and transparent transactions can build trust between communicating devices. A proper trust management system needs to be developed for better security and safer interactions.

5. Identity and access management

Communication between IoT devices and the central server is an essential part of the Internet of Things. Since IoT is a shared ecosystem, a lot of third-party systems and suppliers have access to those sensitive data. A proper identity and access management are needed to be built, to provide adequate access to the right people, and reducing the chances of unauthorized access. The system should be able to differentiate between a real and impersonating identity, detect network sniffers and have proper backup setup, in case of failure.

6. Global standards

Even though IoT is a shared ecosystem of systems from both the private and public sector, no uniform security standards are governing it, as of now. To protect the data and underlying mechanics, all business and industries are developing their own umbrella-level cyber risk paradigms. This has led to the creation of a myriad of standards, which becomes a barrier for interoperability between different system. Closer collaboration with a global standard and governing authority is required for all the systems to interact with each other while maintaining the security.

7. Retrofitting with the existing systems

Most of the companies are trying to implement IoT technology over their current legacy systems, due to its cost effectiveness and reusability, but it also open doors for various security concerns. For one, these legacy systems were built to a standalone system, upgrading them to connect to a shared ecosystem brings many vulnerabilities, due to multiple points of communication, that can also act as a point of failure if proper risk assessment system is not set up. Organizations must accurately access the IoT risk associated, before retrofitting into their systems.

Top 4 security problems that are seen with IoT devices

Howbeit that IOT and cybersecurity threats become a significant trend; vendors, businesses, and individuals need first to understand the necessary insight about IoT related to cybersecurity.

Below, therefore, are challenges facing IoT, and how vendors and businesses can overcome these challenges.

1. Insecure web interface

Generally, the web interface is the interaction between a user and software running on a web server. The web interface built into IoT devices that allow a user to access the device could also allow hackers to gain unauthorized access to the device.

Meanwhile, the downside or the central security weak point that lead to insecure web interface are mostly caused by users when they have weak default credentials, weak account lockout settings, account enumeration and cross-site scripting (XSS).

2. Poor and Insufficient authentication and authorization:

Authentication is the process of verifying a user's access to operate a device, while authorization is the process of allowing an authenticated user to access a device.

However, most users are ignorant when it comes to strengthening the authentication and authorization of their devices; a user should not be allowed to gain much access than usual.

Weak authentication and authorization will easily give cybercriminals an upper hand to operate a device, especially if the user lacks two-factor authentication, password complexity, and role-based access control.

3. Lack of transport encryption

Lack of transport encryption could allow a thief to gain access easily when data is being exchanged with IoT device in an unencrypted format. No wonder why a lot of auto transport companies spend a lot on securing their customer's data before continuing the process of how to ship a car. **4. Insecure cloud interface**

This usually happens when IoT devices use simple security credentials, such as simple passwords or account enumeration.

Chapter 10
How Security Experts
Use IoT

Strategies for protecting IoT

The first step in securing IoT devices is to view them as assets or entities that are open to attacks in multiple ways. It's essential to understand IoT device baseline behavior to be able to identify deviations from established patterns. This enables you to pinpoint rogue activities, such as insider threats for obtaining compromised credentials, accessing sensitive data, and lateral movement within the network.

Because IoT is a hyper-connected, and hyper-distributed collection of resources, many behaviors need to be monitored to keep connected IoT devices in check. It's necessary to understand the pattern of network communication by analyzing network activities such as bytes transmitted per device, the direction of traffic, type of data flow, type of devices being connected, the source of data from devices, and the protocols and services used for data transmission.

Profiling the authorized person(s) who accesses each IoT device provides essential data on its valid use and overall health. For example, user behavior analytics can baseline management and maintenance tasks assigned to personnel, so unusual activities immediately stand out.

Also, if an unknown identity connects through an IoT device to a database server for the first time, being able to identify such activity in real-time can stop an intruder in their tracks.

Cyber Security Considerations for the IoT

With the ever-growing number of connected devices on the market, has come the need for stringent cybersecurity measures to safeguard them. Cybersecurity has always played an important role in technology, but it has taken on an added importance with connected devices. This is because the impact of a cyber attack is no longer limited to one user or device, and can have severe repercussions for an entire network and population.

The expansion of the IoT landscape has paved the way for products to collect more information than ever before. This amount of data collected across the IoT ecosystem underscores the need for a rigorous cybersecurity plan. There have been several examples in recent years of cybercriminals infiltrating connected systems and using that access as a gateway to infiltrate other systems that contained personal information of customers and consumers. It is essential to keep in mind that, although cybercriminals may not want the data that a product collects, they may want the data that a product is connected to.

Protecting a connected device or system requires an understanding of the risks and potential impact of a cyber attack. Conducting a vulnerability assessment allows developers and manufacturers to gain an in-depth knowledge of the potential dangers of their products and how to minimize them without compromising design. This vulnerability assessment will then serve as a guide for implementing the appropriate measures to safeguard the product.

While some may think that a cyber attack only impacts the connected device that is initially infiltrated, cyber attacks can have far-reaching consequences. Infiltration of lighting controls, industrial equipment, and building automation equipment can extend beyond nuisance issues, and an endanger safety. For this reason, it is crucial that cyber-security not be a one-off process. It must be part of an organization's standard operating procedures to protect both the IoT ecosystem and its users. Regular evaluation of products and staying up to date on the latest cybersecurity threats can help ensure continued security.

How cybersecurity experts use the internet of things

No security system is ever going to be perfect. Even if the underlying technology is robust, there will always be the potential for human error to derail the whole thing. It's crucial to understand which threats you're exposed to formulate a response strategy.

Internet of Things is defined as a system of interconnected devices, that communicate with each other, to share information, and derive useful insights from it. A shared ecosystem, while increases the ability to work efficiently, but also brings more vulnerabilities.

With the growing cyber crimes in the field of Internet of Things (IoT), it has become essential to take considerable steps to ensure the security of such environments. While the Cybersecurity system for IoT is still making hits and trying to cope up with current challenges, here are the few ways, it can take steps towards, to ensure, better safety to IoT network:

1) Zero-trust security with Blockchain

With the emergence of Blockchain technology, it gained widespread acknowledgment from all fields, due to its transparency and security. Blockchain works on a distributed ledger, that records all transaction, that is created and distributed, and is shared with all users. Such transparency makes it impossible for counterfeiting recorded sales or tampering. This can be an invaluable asset for Cybersecurity system, by keeping information safe, like user identities, messages, logs, and making it difficult to brute force or 'hack' into such devices of the system.

Zero-trust security is a system, in which no devices trust each other, and authentication is always required, to verify each other. Such mechanisms might add a slight overhead to its performance but adds a great deal to its security. Validating it every time makes it almost impossible to sniff into one's communication channel, or impersonate as a trusted system. Blockchain can be used to build smart contracts for devices communication, that will enable interactions without a prior defined trust relationship. This will make the system resources and transactions more auditable and less prone to attack, due to the compromised system. It would not only prevent outside attacks but also reduce the chances of inside attacks(sniffers or compromised system in a network).

2) Artificial intelligence and Machine Learning in IoT

While Artificial Intelligence and Machine Learning are primarily used to make intelligent decisions for IoT to optimize resources usage, but it can also improve the security of such networks. IoT collects a massive amount of data, which is then crunched by AI systems, to find patterns and provide feedback for its proper functioning. These data can also help predict user's behavior, and find out potential threats, also known as Predictive policing. Such technology can prevent future attacks, and find the perpetrator before it happens. While the system may not be able to avoid every cyber attack, but it can help an organization gets insights on its potential flaws, and work towards rectifying it.

Artificial Intelligence and Machine Learning can also automate the security protocols for the IoT system, and can guaranty impartiality towards the system checks, thanks to zero human interventions. It can implement bots to ping though all the networks and communication channels, to ensure that no devices are compromised at any time. Due to the evolving nature of AI, it is difficult for any third party to predict the system checks and sniff into a secure system, undetected. Such bots can not only do silent system checks but can also take preventive actions, to stop malicious activities, on behalf of human administrators.

3) Open Web Application Security Project (OWASP)

With the rate of adoption of IoT devices, there isn't a single security standard, or a governing community to set the guidelines for the IoT system. Most of the companies implement their cybersecurity standard, as of now, to protect themselves from cybercrimes but in doing so, reduces the interoperability of the systems, due to standards mismatch.

One way to ensure similarities between standards is to follow the Open Web Application Security Project (OWASP), which elaborates the security issues related to IoT and provides a set of guidelines/best practices that should be followed to avoid any vulnerabilities in the system while adopting or upgrading it to IoT infrastructure. OWASP IoT provides a list of attack surfaces and standards to enable organizations to access security risks, related to such systems, and how to ensure the security of the network.

4) Lightweight IoT Security

Pervasive IoT systems are more at risk of cyber attacks due to limited resources, and minimal network security. IoT devices are built to be energy efficient. Hence they don't contain a lot of performance firepower, to provide a fully secure system. Thus, for such devices, light-weight security systems come in handy. These lightweight systems can handle authentication, key exchanges, and access control, without utilizing too many resources. One such example of a lightweight authentication system is WiFi Hallow, used for low-rate and long-range IoT applications. Since these devices are not powerful, the lightweight mechanism needs to make sure, that it focuses on meeting the specific requirements, rather than providing all over protection. Various such mechanism can be put into place, to ensure all requirements are covered up, without adding overhead to the processing power.

5) Active Cyber Defense

Most of the cybersecurity system like authentication, encryption, access controls are passive defenses, which tries to prevent the attackers from breaking in. They do not help in analyzing the patterns to actively fighting the intruders. Active cyber defense like Deception based cyber system sets up random changes in network security, making it difficult for attackers to hack in to, lure them to pre-deployed honeypots. Honeypots traps are virtual devices, which acts as a part of the system but are closely monitored by system admins, so if an attacker gets lured into one, then the organization can find out more about the hacker's behavior, and the weak spots in their system, through which they reached the entry.

A deception-based cyber system can also set up multiple fake credentials, to access the system. These fake credentials, if used by a hacker to gain access, can be closely monitored, find their patterns, and help fortify the security system, by identifying the flaw in the system.

6) Naming conventions other than IP addresses

All the devices including IoT devices use IPv4 and IPv6 for naming conventions, to distinguish themselves from other, and or communication. Even though it increases the interoperability between the system, but it also becomes relatively more comfortable for hackers to impersonate another device in the system, and gain access. To avoid it, IoT devices should a different naming convention like Host Identity Protocol (HIP), to interact with each other. This will distinguish IoT devices from other devices and will use host identities, instead of an IP address. They will share cryptographic keys to enable communication with each other. This will ensure that no device outside the network can directly access or communicate with IoT devices, making it safer, reducing the chances of an attack.

While these solutions can surely provide the answers for the much-needed security upgrade for IoT systems, but it will take quite some time, before those can be adequately researched and deployed. Till then, Manufacturers and organizations have to set up their cybersecurity paradigm, while following the necessary standards, provided by OWASP.

Cybersecurity Must Evolve to Deal With Threats

This means, in simple terms, that cybersecurity will come down to a continually evolving defense strategy that prevents hackers from controlling your everyday tasks. Our collective reliance on technology is not a bad thing, but, is highly exploitable.

We must remember always to be smart about how we store our passwords and how loosely we share our data with companies. Diligence is half of the cybersecurity, and the other half is welcoming incoming technologies that will assist us in protecting data and developing software. There is no shortage of malware out there.

We must always remember that persistence is critical and that innovation unlocks change. IoT has created a world in which every part of our lives can be accessed illegally. While this is seen as a frightening prospect to many, the truth is that keen eyes typically thwart exploits.

However, in recent times, we have had massive successful hacking endeavors such as the Equifax hack and the Target hack.

These brought cybersecurity to the forefront of our minds as we panicked about the future of our information and what constant interconnectivity truly means. We must not let this dissuade us from our collective efforts and should by no means stall our progress in the name of false safety. In truth, large corporations are the biggest targets, and many individuals are often spared in such attacks.

Cybersecurity and IoT Companies Will Have to Work Together

Cybersecurity, however, will have to evolve to meet the new security demands brought on by IoT. Now a company must account for interconnected camera systems, telephones, automobiles, and even refrigerators.

Full faith can be granted to these cybersecurity companies if we not only use practical common sense but have a continuous goal of safety as a whole. Having a phone that can control our house or a personal assistant that can schedule our meetings has made life much easier and should never be thrown away due to fear.

Security companies have quite a lot on their plate as the IoT and cybersecurity technologies continuously advance. In the parallels are hackers who are continually creating new bugs and exploits to crash systems and steal data.

The difficulty then, for cybersecurity companies, is creating tools that will protect all of the different devices that are now integral to an individual's life. There are no more households with just one computer or a person with just one internet connected device.

There is the need to protect the millions upon millions of devices that are used every second of the day, and that job alone is both impressive and tremendous. For cybersecurity Professionals everywhere, the task may seem daunting, but it is manageable and will be controlled one day.

IoT has come to change the way individuals, businesses, and communities interact. It is evident that IoT is making changes to our daily lives and work lives. Different opportunities now exist for individuals and companies via the integration and collaboration of technology.

With each passing day, different innovations are making their way into our lives but at the same time, along with these technological innovations are cyber threats with posing an exceptional level of risk to individuals and businesses. When it comes to IoT, there is a need for Cybersecurity to be on its A-game if IoT will fulfill its noble purpose.

In just a matter of time, sensing and visualization tools will be birthed by the IoT, and these tools and much more will be made available to people, at any time, and anywhere, and on any device on both an individual, business, cooperate or even community level. The ease with which information is shared through the IoT makes individuals and organizations open to cyber threats, and as it stands in as much as IoT offers huge benefits, there is still the growing risks of threats.

IoT provides a vast platform for both personal and business growth and innovation, but there is the need to know the potential risk that is involved, in other for more sustainable solutions to be birthed.

As IoT continues to expand, and with more and more devices or machines being utilized as an interacting medium by individuals and cooperate bodies, there is the need for this personnel to adapt and understand that cyber threats would always be in the horizon, but having a fully functional Cybersecurity framework offers a competitive advantage. Not only will individuals and organizations benefit considerably by the various opportunities provided by the digital world, but they will also be able to limit exposure to risk, and also minimize the cost of having to deal with them.

Part 3
Blockchain

Chapter 11
What is a Bitcoin?

What is a Bitcoin? What is a Blockchain?

The block chain that started it all – also known as Bitcoin is now considered an arguably ingenious invention by an individual or group of people under the moniker Satoshi Nakamoto. Block-string technology is one of the fundamental concepts of most cryptomohedral systems. What it does is record a set of details that include time, a cryptographic signature binding the sender, and some data that can represent just about anything. In the case of Bitcoin, it is the number of bitcoins being sent, but could be a digital cryptographic signature, called a hash, of any electronic document.

The block chain is constantly growing, because each time a block is completed, a new block is generated. Blocks are linked to each other (such as a string) in an appropriate linear and chronological order, with each block containing a hash of the previous block. Each computer connected to the Bitcoin network using a client that performs the task of validating and passing on the transactions receives a copy of the block chain, which is automatically downloaded when connecting to the Bitcoin network. The complete copy of the block chain has records of each Bitcoin transaction already executed.

But where does the blockchain come from? Its origin lies in a long-discussed problem of digital currencies: how to make sure that a "digital coin" is actually spent only once? The decentralized Blockchain no longer needs an institution in the middle that checks and releases the transactions and thus ensures that nobody manipulates and cheats.

Why "decentralized" is so important and revolutionary becomes perhaps clear when one draws a parallel to the analogue world. If you pay for something in a shop with your credit or debit card, you have at least one middleman in between, and often several. They earn money from each transaction and, last but not least, it is precisely understandable who paid what and when to whom. In addition, it needs accounts, so that the transaction can take place at all. The situation is different with cash: This changes directly its owner - from the purse to the cash register. Nobody is in between. Nobody branches off fees. Nobody has power over the payment process. Nobody needs to know the names of people who have spent and taken the money. Even accounts are not necessary for cash to work.

The inventor of the blockchain is called Satoshi Nakamoto, but he or she has never made himself public. There were always messages, the person behind the Blockchain was unmasked. But that does not seem to be the case today. Anyway, it soon became clear that a blockchain can not only be used for a cryptocurrency like Bitcoin, but also for other fields of application. And in the next step came with Ethereum the automations added.

An introduction to Blockchain

The 'chain of blocks' is seen as the main technological innovation of Bitcoin, as it serves as a voucher for all transactions in the network. The technology can work for just about any type of transaction involving values, including money, assets and properties. Their potential uses are almost unlimited: from tax collection to the possibility that immigrants send money back to their families in countries where banking is difficult.

Let's compare common banking transactions with transactions on the Bitcoin network to paint a better picture of what all this means. Banks and account systems use records and legers to track and record transaction times. The difference is that the block chain is completely decentralized and open source. This means that people do not have to rely on or trust the central bank to track transactions. Peer-to-peer blockchain technology can keep track of all transactions without the fear of erasing them or corrupting the leger.

"**Transactions**" may or may not have something to do with some form of currency like Bitcoin when discussing Blockchain technology. Rather, it is generally about transferring data from A to B without causing copies.

An important feature of Blockchain is how the information is stored. This also explains the name "block chain": The transactions are stored in blocks and these blocks in turn contain encrypted information about the previous blocks. The result is a chain that goes back to the very first block. It is most typically explained as a general ledger in which transactions are recorded and each page (or in this case block) contains a checksum of the previous pages. This general ledger exists in the case of Blockchain purely digitally and is kept decentralized multiple times.

Another essential feature of Blockchain is the word "decentralized" used above. This means that it can function without a central intermediary, without a person, company, or institution that stores and authenticates the transactions. Instead, the information is kept up-to-date throughout the network using the benefits of a peer-to-peer network. This allows users the ability to feel confident that things are going right.

Another and still quite new feature arise from the digital nature of the information. This digital nature creates the ability to have simultaneous conditions and 'if x, then y' statements. Let's take the Bitcoin example and say that the transactions in a blockchain represent a kind of means of payment. In this way, you could specify for which purposes the amount may be used or whether it will be returned to the sender after a certain date. Theoretically, this could be used, among other things, in companies for budgets and forecasting. Or a government agency could decide that a housing subsidy can actually only be spent on rent.

So why is blockchain technology so tantalizing to use as a currency in the Internet of Things? Machines easily know who/what paid and what that was paid to on a leger that is incorruptible. The internet of things is creating an excessive amount of data, and when your Google Dot can order your anything you want off of amazon via voice commands, you need to have an accurate leger to record every transaction to protect the consumer from fraud. A human intervention would no longer be necessary to keep this process 'safe'. This is also where "Smart Contracts" come into play: for example, anyone who generates solar power on the roof of their private home could offer and sell excess automatically – it allows everyone on the network an ability to transact in ways they never had been able to previously.

There is no doubt that blockchain technology will become conventional. The level of interest being shown by this technology demonstrates its potential to enable the development of applications that will bring new approaches to old business problems. It is the social, legal, and financial challenges brought about by these changes that may be a much more difficult problem to solve.

There are three main types of Blockchain:

Public: Transactions are publicly available and the system is fully decentralized.

Private: Controlled by a single organization, which also regulates the registration fee and channel entries. This version can potentially deviate from the original concept's ethic because it suppresses decentralization. However, when it is implemented on several sites and data centers, it retains the dimension of decentralization.

Allowed: This is a hybrid type between the public and private version of the Blockchain. It looks like a system run by a consortium, with no organization taking control. In doing so, this version offers partial decentralization.

Chapter 12
The Revolution of
How We Trust

Blockchain: The revolution of trust

With Blockchain, the user no longer has to question whether or not to trust the middleman, simply because the middleman does not exist and the network is decentralized. This decentralization makes it possible to record the history of the transactions that are carried out in the network on a user-to-user or peer-to-peer basis, which makes any manipulation of the data impossible without all users on the network becoming aware. In terms of application, any verification measure such as a notarial act could, for example, be carried out through a blockchain in an automated and decentralized manner. We move from a trust-based model, as we know it, to a model where trust is delegated to an algorithm, that is, to the underlying technology.

The main objective of the blockchain's first application, bitcoin, is to exchange value between peers without intermediary. This exchange of value can thus be done without any fear of decisions going against the interested parties.

If the blockchain allows a better relationship between individuals, in the case of companies, it can also allow optimizing contractual relations. In the financial sector, some large banks such as UBS, BNY Mellon, Deustche Bank, Santander have joined an effort to study currencies that could be used in interbank payment processes and with their customers. Other financial groups are interested in virtual currencies that have similar properties to bitcoin. In addition, central banks such as the US Federal Reserve, the ECB, the Bank of England, the People's Bank of China, the Bank of Japan or the Bank of Canada are exploring the possibilities offered by blockchain networks, in the perspective of eventually replace fiduciary currencies with digital currencies. The growing scale of the phenomenon that the blockchain has the power to revolutionize the existing system.

With all of this having been said, a fundamental question remains unanswered: **What model of governance should be applied to the blockchain?**

An analysis of the governance models at work highlights, despite the possible variations according to the situations, three common characteristics: *decentralization* (no regulation is operated by an operator), *autonomous financing* (these governance models are not on a financial regulatory system such as financial institutions), and *trust* (the transaction is not based on a trusted third party unlike a traditional payment via a bank, for example). This analysis also highlights some of the improvements that need to be considered for the future, at the risk of some disillusionment from both industry leaders and governing bodies.

To understand the situation in which the governance of the block-chain is, several examples can be presented here, including the models Dash and Decred.

Decentralization

The Dash model illustrates a use case of decentralized governance that is both relevant and controversial. This is based on a decentralized node with autonomous financing, around a node connected to a network from which transactions and exchanges are made via software connected to said network 24 hours a day, 7 days a week, 365 days a year. In August 2015, for the first time, a system of governance was created in a decentralized way: this is the main feature of Dash.

The Decred project is also an example of decentralized governance, but it has some peculiarities compared to the previous model of Dash. The long-term goal is to create a cryptocurrency. Unlike Dash, it is not based on a "network-actor" pair, but on the algorithmic systems of "proof of stake" (PoS) and "proof of work" (PoW). Since it is managed only by algorithms, this model is totally decentralized. Decred is a more simplified program than Dash, and its users can vote to express their dissatisfaction or not. In a way, Decred "delegates" governance to users, called minors, to improve its functioning. For that, it integrates their remarks in the blockchain, PoS, and PoW algorithms in order to allow the to balance these requests to obtain a more robust consensus. and its users can vote to express their dissatisfaction or not. In a way, Decred "delegates" governance to users, called minors, to improve its functioning. For that, it integrates their remarks in the blockchain and the PoS and PoW algorithms allow the balancing of these requests to obtain a more robust consensus.

These two models account for two distinct types of strategy for governing a cryptocurrency. The first strategy highlights the key role of the network-actor couple (the masternodes and the minors), while the second emphasizes the algorithms with a long-term approach. Both approaches have limitations. Bipolar governance leads to neglecting other stakeholders, such as users who have no decision-making and informational power. We thus find ourselves in the schema of the theory of the agency with problems of information asymmetry. Moreover, if the second model proposed, that of Decred, is interesting for the agents "risk-adverse" (that is to say, hostile to the risk), it is unsuitable for the so-called risky agents, that is to say, for example, those who are not afraid to invest with a high-risk potential.

Based on this observation, we can highlight several key points in the governance model applied to cryptocurrency. First of all, all users should be considered by means of rewards. The model envisaged must indeed be multi-actors and decentralized, with no potential takeover of one actor over the other. It is also a question of considering a vision both in the short and the long term, in order to answer all the agents, "risk-adverse" or not.

Smart Contracts

One of the applications of blockchain, based on computerized trust management, is the "smart contract", or a computer protocol for verifying, monitoring and applying the negotiation and execution of a contract. However, according to the vast majority of industry experts, a business can be summed up as a "knot of contracts and relationships". In this way, the goal is to distribute these contracts fairly between the principal and the agent. Unlike the current model of corporate governance - where there are opportunistic behaviors - the blockchain responds as a fair equalizer, to stifle any opportunism. The blockchain being a transparent register, verifiable by all actors, opportunism according to many of the sceptics have since retorted.

The automation of governance mechanisms via smart contracts, the elimination of opportunism, as well as lower transaction costs make blockchain governance what many users and blockchain advocates describe as a more effective governance model. However, this governance model has at least one substantial limitation. Despite the guarantees of integrity blockchain boasts, many skeptics argue that it is impossible to truly check and verify the trustworthiness of everything utilizing blockchain – while it is difficult, there are ways to tamper with several blockchains.

The blockchain is not just an additional new technology emerging on the scene, but a disruptive technology that is shaking up all traditional modes of governance. However, there is the fact – that this truly is of a mode of governance that until now has not existed. Because of this, businesses and governments must take into account a number of considerations at the organizational, managerial, and financial levels before implementing this technology.

Chapter 13
Practical Uses for Blockchain

Practical Uses for Blockchain We See Today

Rights management in all of its multitude of forms is a topic of many startups. Imagine downloading a piece of music that incorporates your private copying right over a blockchain. Now you can distribute it to five friends, but then the song itself knows that your quota has been exhausted. At the same time, the settlement of royalties for the artists could be organized within a blockchain, without the need for a collecting entity. With this model it would organize itself instead. The payouts could theoretically be done independently. In short, everything about Digital Rights Management is a big field with many, many use cases. Whether this is a use case that is actually implemented and adopted is another question – however undoubtedly, an extremely interesting theoretical use case that is truthfully just one of many.

Another area of application with a lot of potential is logistics. The port of Rotterdam, for example, launched a project last year to map freight documents in a blockchain. The goal is to digitize the entire process. This is an ambitious project in an industry that has been somewhat traditionally resistant to embracing the emerging technologies and that's why it's so exciting. It would be a huge gain in efficiency for the specifically the port industry worldwide if this gets implemented.

The subject of 'e-Government' is a blockchain topic that is worthy of its own book. You could replace land registers with a blockchain system. You can map citizen directories via Blockchain. Whenever transactions need to be documented, this is an ideal application scenario. Remember – **blockchain is a revolution in the way we trust. Anywhere trust is valued is an opportunity to implement a blockchain solution.**

Another industry that is begging for the advent of a blockchain revolution is the energy industry. There is the idea of a completely decentralized energy market and its production/distribution. The focal point is that you no longer have a large producer and a large network operator on one side (decentralization), and on the current model we use we have the customers who can only participate as a purchaser of energy. Instead, imagine a system in which each solar panel could be bolted on the roof and automatically provide excess electricity through a smart contract. This would allow participants of this system the ability to buy, sell, and trade energy throughout the network. Of course, it still needs someone to run the infrastructure, so this isn't a one-hundred percent decentralized model, but the transactions could be represented by the blockchain.

The encryption also makes Blockchain a phenomenal tool to prevent money laundering. The completed contracts are completely transparent and the technology allows you to make the most accurate records of which transactions were made to the various participants. Through the possible identification and verification of their own customers using a blockchain leger, it is possible actively to prevent money laundering.

Due to the secure and nature of Blockchain to be tamper-proof, it is a useful tool to handle accounting, among all forms of finance. Since there is extremely small possibility for errors, the integrity of the data and the traceability is given a gold standard of trust. Also special is the immutability of the technology. Once a transaction has been made, it cannot be changed, not even by the people who created those entries. Of course, the disadvantage of this use is that jobs like auditors can become superfluous, and the workforce will have to create different jobs for intermediary members.

Blockchain and Smart Contracts are a major application for those in the insurance industry as well. Contracts and the settlement of claims can be regulated transparently. All contracts and all claims for damages would be managed by the network and filter out incorrect or fraudulent claims for damages. For example, it would no longer be possible to obtain multiple claims for damages from one client for the same case. Blockchain is a means for stripping frauds and scammers of the tools they use to steal money.

In the health sector, since the blockchain can be set up so that only certain people have access to the data and you can still use the world-wide network to store the data, it is perfectly suited to store sensitive data. Thus, patient records, disease histories, reports and much more can be stored in the blockchain and only then unlocked for someone, if they are allowed to get this information. Currently, individual data-bases are created, in so-called silos, which are mutually shielded and only forwarded on special request. This leads to inconsistent data and can also lead to problems in the treatment.

It would also be possible, for example, to connect special devices with their own patient profile and thus create an interactive medical record. For example, the blood glucose and insulin pump readings could be automatically matched to the file and adjusted by the physician as needed.

Blockchain can be used in three ways: as Public, Private or Consortium Blockchain.

The public blockchain is a thoroughly decentralized network without a parent instance, as is the case with most popular crypto currencies. Each transaction is verified and synchronized by each node of the blockchain before it is written to the system. This makes this variant relatively slow and very resource-intensive, but transparent and secure.

In private blockchain, a company operates the system and owns the sovereignty over the transactions. It verifies and writes as the only participant every transaction in the system. In addition, the reading rights for the transactions per user can be restricted, which allows higher data protection than the public version. Because the size of the private blockchain is limited by company boundaries, the resource requirements and the processing time per transaction are also limited. However, abandoning the completely decentralized approach also destroys part of the reliability.

The consortium blockchain is a kind of private and public hybrid. Here, a group of participants share the power to decide on the verification and distribution of the read rights of transactions. This offers many advantages of private blockchain such as efficiency and privacy of transactions without putting all sovereignty in one hand.

Chapter 14
Blockchain and Cybersecurity

Blockchain and Cyber Security

At a time when the digitization of society is becoming more and more advanced, a corollary threat is increasing its scope: **Cyber-crime**. Indeed, hackers, frauds, and nefarious parties use increasingly sophisticated and advanced techniques with the aim of stealing many value-added data such as banking data and health data. The recent onslaught of ransomware cases confirms this trend towards the sophistication of the techniques used to obtain data and hold data hostage. With malware coupled with cryptography, it becomes almost too simple to block access to all files of from access to anyone aside from the hacker. The hackers then ask the user to pay a ransom in order to recover the normal use of their servers and data.

Incidentally, most ransomware attacks require the user to pay in some type of cryptocurrency, bitcoin being the most prominently seen.

What is the blockchain doing in this story?

As we know, any technology can have many potential applications. Cybersecurity is one of them. Indeed, it could improve cyber defense by being a platform for preventing fraudulent activities through consensus mechanisms. The blockchain could also detect falsification of data through its underlying characteristics such as operational resilience, data encryption, auditability, transparency and immutability. With that having been said, the understanding of this theme is far from easy, and even seasoned cybersecurity experts are having trouble understand what blockchain's role in cybersecurity will be when all is said and done.

The key point that asserts that blockchain technology is a chance for cybersecurity is its infallible character. While a centralized server suggests porous entries for the joy of the most experienced hackers, a distributed server is, instead, a reinforced wall not easily penetrated. Unless it has almost infinite power, it is, to date, impossible to inject malware into a blockchain leger.

Let's summarize some of the key benefits that could bring the blockchain to cybersecurity.

Authentication without recourse to the human factor

With blockchain technology, companies would be able to authenticate devices and users without the need for a password. This would eliminate human intervention from the authentication process, thus preventing it from becoming a potential attack vector.

The use of a centralized architecture and simple connections is the great weakness of conventional systems in production today. No matter how much an organization invests in cybersecurity, all these efforts are completely futile if employees and customers use passwords that are easy to steal or hack (the famous 123456). As stated earlier in this book, cybersecurity starts with education. Because users are the single biggest threat to any company's data, the blockchain solution would provide strong authentication and resolution of a single point of attack at the same time.

With the help of the blockchain, a security system used in an organization could take advantage of a distributed public key infrastructure for device and user authentication. This security system would provide each device with a specific Secure Sockets Layer (SSL) certificate instead of a more vulnerable password. The management of the certificate data would then be carried out on the blockchain, which would make it practically impossible for the hackers to use false certificates.

Unique and irreversible traceability

Each transaction added to a private or public blockchain is timestamped and digitally signed, and irreversibly. This is one of the basic principles of technology. This means that companies can trace to a given period for each transaction and locate the corresponding part on the blockchain via their public address.

This characteristic is to be compared to what is commonly called non-repudiation. It means that the author of a statement will not have the opportunity to positively question the authorship of that statement or the validity of an associated contract. The term is often used in a legal framework where the authenticity of a signature is disputed. In such a case, the authenticity is said to be "repudiated". In practice, when a contract is signed on the internet, it cannot be challenged by one of the parties. A blockchain would greatly increase the reliability of the system since each transaction would then be cryptographically associated with a user. Non-repudiation would become null and void.

Any new transaction added to a blockchain causes the registry to be transformed. This implies that with each new iteration of the system, the previous state will be stored, which will result in a fully traceable and irreversible history.

The blockchain audit capability provides businesses with a level of security and transparency at each iteration. From a cybersecurity perspective, this would provide entities with an additional level of assurance that the data has not been tampered with and that it is authentic.

Decentralized storage, stronger than the cloud

Some might be tempted to compare the blockchain to cloud computing. Indeed, in both cases, you can access a program without having to actually have it on your machine. However, the difference is fundamental: if, in cloud computing, access to documents is certified by a trusted third party storing data on centralized servers, the blockchain distributes all documents on all computers in the network that own then all a copy of the documents, or rather originals certified by the technique of the aforementioned timestamp.

Blockchain users must maintain their data on their computer in their network. Because of this, they can make sure that the chain will not collapse. For example, if a person who does not own a data component, such as a hacker, tries to modify a block, the entire system examines each block of data to locate the one that differs from the rest. If this type of block is located by the system, the disputed block is simply excluded from the chain, recognizing it as false.

The blockchain is designed so that the storage location or the central authority does not exist. The most topical and well-known example is the bitcoin blockchain. On the network, each user has a role to play in the storage of all or part of the blockchain. Each network member is responsible for checking shared and / or maintained data to ensure that existing data cannot be deleted and false data cannot be added.

Blockchain against DDoS

As mentioned earlier in this book, the denial-of-service attack distributed (DDoS - Distributed Denial of Service attack) is a computer attack from several sources and making it unavailable service. DDoS thus prevents users from using the service. Today, DDoS are some of the most difficult attacks to fight. But a blockchain could be the exact remedy the problem calls for.

Blockchain transactions can be easily denied if participating units are prevented from sending transactions. For example, a DDoS attack against a set of entities or an entity can paralyze the entire backing infrastructure and blockchain organization. Such attacks could introduce integrity risks for the blockchain, causing the blockchain to shut it down.

At present, the difficulty in preventing DDoS attacks comes from the existing system of domain names. The implementation of blockchain technology would completely decentralize the DNS, distributing the content to a larger number of nodes, making it almost impossible to hack hackers. A system such as this can ensure that it is invulnerable to hackers by using block strings to protect the data, unless each node is cleaned at the same time.

Blockchain technology is here to stay. It will help us protect businesses, individuals and governments from cyber-attacks. The innovative use of the blockchain is already becoming a component of other domains, far beyond cryptocurrencies, and can be primarily useful for improving cybersecurity.

Hackers can block networks, manipulate data, lure users into cyber-traps, steal identities, and lead other malicious attacks by taking advantage of centralized data repositories and single points of failure (SPOF). This is where the technology of blockchain promises wonders with its principle of decentralized management. The decentralized management spreads that single point of failure out into a redundant, resilient network of peers.

Blockchain technology is a powerful tool in the arsenal of Cybersecurity to counter certain types of cybercrime. The decentralized aspect of the technology is the key to security and confidentiality, from securing data transactions to minimizing information sharing and protecting the individual use of IoT devices.

Building on the Blockchain of Identity Systems, the Internet of Things and important infrastructures could therefore solve some of the biggest problems of cybercrime today.

Chapter 15
How Security Experts use Blockchain

How Cybersecurity Experts Use Blockchain

Hackers penetrating networks and accessing precious private data is a global crisis that is growing every year as the connectivity of individuals and devices increases (explosion of the connected objects market –(IoT), development of smart cities and mass digitization of the population). There is no longer a single week that passes by without new stories and reports about computer attacks, data leaks or new "ransomware". Even though the public, Internet and telecommunications sectors are the main targets of cyberattacks, data piracy affects all categories of businesses ranging from small businesses to web giants. We need to keep in mind the impressive attack suffered by TV5 Monde which almost ended in a hacking of hackers or massive data leaks at web giants such as Linkedin, Yahoo etc. is just one of many high-profile hacks. There are hundreds of thousands of smaller, unreported hacks that happen every day.

It is difficult to estimate the losses due to the various computer attacks but according to estimates of many cyber security consulting companies, the losses would be of the order of 13 billion dollars for all worms and viruses and $ 226 billion for attacks. According to other studies, cybercrime is expected to cost $ 6 trillion a year by 2021.

In their attempts to protect against computer attacks, companies face several problems:

- There is a shortage of protection solutions that are proactive in identifying new threats.

- Cyber-attacks are constantly evolving which makes setting up a very complicated protection policy. In addition, this requires security experts and (very) important financial resources.

- Current cybersecurity solutions rely on an isolated and personalized approach to threat management, with (very) limited (or no) knowledge sharing between industry players.

- Most of the patterns and signatures that help security software detect a vulnerability are available for free on the Internet, allowing hackers to have the same knowledge as a security consultant.

The consequence is a game of cat and mouse where everyone tries to be in the forefront in order to protect themselves for the companies and to learn from the example of the first victim of any given attack. In this unfortunate model, the cybersecurity measures are exclusively reactive, not proactive.

It is in this context that Cybersecurity experts create a solution based on blockchain, smart contracts and Artificial Intelligence to enable companies to protect themselves at a lower cost while always having a lead over the pirates.

This may be achieved by the use of Uncloak. Uncloak is just one of many cybersecurity tools, based on the blockchain and the use of smart contracts, which aims to help companies avoid being hacked that are becoming more and more common in today's technology industry. For this, Uncloak aims to give users the ability to sort through "cyber jargon" and understand it which will correct and solve security problems. In addition to this, the solution is intended to be proactive (and more reactive) in the protection against computer attacks.

Chapter 16
Advantages and
Disadvantages of Blockchain

Advantages of the use of blockchain in cybersecurity

Here are what are widely considered to be the main advantages of the use of Blockchain technology in relation to cybersecurity:

Decentralization: Thanks to the peer-to-peer network, an external verification is not necessary, since each user can observe the network transactions.

Tracking: All transactions made in Blockchains are digitally signed and have a temporary stamp, so that users of the network can easily track the transaction history, while they can track the accounts at any historical moment. Also, this feature allows a company to obtain valid information about assets or product distribution.

Confidentiality: the confidentiality of network members is high thanks to public key cryptography that authenticates users and encrypts their transactions.

Security in relation to fraud: in case of hacking, it is easy to define a malicious behavior thanks to peer-to-peer connections and distributed consensus. To this day, Blockchains are considered "impossible to hack", since to make an impact on a network, attackers must take control of 51% of the nodes of the same.

Sustainability: Blockchain technology does not have a single point of vulnerability, which means that, even in the case of DDoS attacks, the system will function normally thanks to the multiple copies of the accounting book.

Integrity: the distributed accounting book guarantees the protection of the data against any modification or destruction. In addition, the technology guarantees the authenticity and irreversibility of the transactions carried out. The encrypted blocks contain immutable data resistant to hacking.

Resilience: the peer-to-peer nature of this technology guarantees that the network will work at all times even if some nodes are disconnected or are being attacked. In the event of an attack, a company can make certain nodes redundant and, in this way, can operate as usual.

Data quality: Blockchain technology cannot improve the quality of the data, but it can guarantee the accuracy and quality of the data after they have been encrypted in the Blockchain.

Smart contracts: software programs that are based on the ledger. These programs guarantee the execution of the contractual terms and verify the parts. The Blockchain technology can significantly increase the security standards with regard to smart contracts, since it minimizes the risks of errors and cyber-attacks.

Availability: there is no need to store sensitive data in a single site, since the Blockchain technology allows multiple copies of the data that are always available to the users of the network.

Increased customer confidence: your customers will trust your company more if you can guarantee a high level of security in terms of data. On the other hand, Blockchain technology allows to provide customers with information about the company's products and services instantaneously.

Disadvantages of the use of blockchain in cybersecurity

Irreversibility: in case a user loses or forgets the private key to decrypt them, there is a risk that the encrypted data will be unrecoverable.

Storage limits: each block can contain a maximum of 1 Mb of data and, on average, a Blockchain can only manage 7 transactions per second.

Risk of cyber-attacks: although this technology greatly reduces the risk of malicious intervention, it is not a panacea against all cyber-threats. If the attackers manage to exploit most of the network, it is possible that the entire database will be lost.

Main Obstacles of Blockchain and Cybersecurity

It is extremely important today moreso than ever, we need to put aside technological advances and think about the human side of things. There are some very legitimate issues can arise in the areas of policy, certification and regulation. In addition, several thousand hours of custom software design and upstream and downstream programming are still needed to link the new blockchain registers to the existing business networks. Although no one can change the information contained in the blockchain, they might be able to use the IP address with which you access your blockchain wallet and hack your device. That's why VPN providers offer a great way to enhance your security when dealing with sensitive information.

It's not as easy as a magic wand, because in order for everything to work perfectly and seamlessly, the distributed leger must be able to communicate with other elements of the process seamlessly. The blockchain should allow faster installation, configuration, and reso-lution of problems. Achieving these gains in efficiency must be easy and cheap enough for all parties to seize and benefit from.

Security is also a concern. Banks are not interested in an open model of identity. Banks and regulators want to be able to exercise tight control. The development of a unique digital identity passport will be a crucial step.

Regulation is also essential to creating an open digital environment for trade and financial transactions. Current physical certificates need to be digitized to take full advantage of a fully electronic system. In addition to the concerns already expressed, we must consider other barriers to the full adoption of these technologies, and find the right answers to the questions that surround regulation.

Who will take primary responsibility for maintaining and managing the blockchain?

What about the admission of new participants to the blockchain?

In terms of transactions - who is turning to validate them and who determines their visibility?

Given the incredible opportunity for decentralization, blockchain technology offers the opportunity to create businesses and activities that are both flexible and secure. With the blockchain, we can imagine a world in which contracts are embedded in a digital code and stored in transparent and shared databases, where they are protected against deletion, falsification and modification.

In this world, every agreement, process, task, and payment would have a digital record and signature that could be identified, validated, stored, and shared. Individuals, organizations, machines and algorithms interact freely with each other without conflict. This is the huge potential of the blockchain.

Key Cybersecurity Concerns

Regardless of the fact that the application of blockchain for companies and governments is still far from gained in terms of global recognition, what is undeniable is that it has the potential to create new foundations for the systems economic and social issues. The process of implementation will be gradual and regular, not sudden, as the waves of technological and institutional change take hold. This view and its strategic implications are what we will explore as a community that adapts to this innovative disrupter to the technology market.

While one can easily identify the obvious advantages of the blockchain in terms of the decentralized environment, there are other palatable advantages blockchain has to accompany security measures, and ensuring the integrity of databases.

Everything would be perfect if we did not take into account some obstacles in the area of management, responsibility, constant evolution and the increasing volume of data, capacity problems, confirmation etc.

Nothing is Safe, But It Could Happen

Since its initial appearance, the evolution of the blockchain may be slow but steady and is now being tested in virtually every conceivable area, from travel to medicine and beyond. When it comes to cyber technologies, security and protection are of paramount importance.

The blockchain's potential for security applications is considerable because the very essence of this technology makes it the perfect foundation for cybersecurity.

One of the things that is changing with security and protection in the digital world are the dangers and hacking attempts of anything that contains valuable data. Because of this, the virtual (but very real) threats evolve at the same pace and adapt accordingly.

What we should also agree on is that the human side of things when it comes to mistakes and miscalculations is the number one factor in cybersecurity. The blockchain solves this problem successfully, easily and reliably, so it is essential to consider how we can best use the potential of the blockchain to use it in real-world security applications. To enhance this security, you will need to add additional layers of protection: A good VPN, a good anti-virus, and an operating system updated with all the latest security protocols.

Data Security Permanently

As cryptocurrencies continue to populate the tech scene, security of cryptocurrencies and the blockchain leger in general is at the forefront, as the technology industry has always been focused on protecting customer data. This is even more significant when the data is very sensitive and valuable (medical records, financial information).

Cyber-attacks make it possible to obtain such documents and use them without authorization. This is especially true given that in many cases the data could have been easily protected had the victims taken cybersecurity more seriously. Blockchain technology has already been used in this regard to ensure the security of financial transactions by allowing the transparency of transactions that cannot be modified, altered, moved and / or deleted. All parties involved can rely on this technology before, during and after transactions.

The same approach could be used for storing sensitive information. The blockchain records everything and does not allow the manipulation of the data, let alone without it being clearly indicated to the hosts / parties concerned. The logical conclusion is that when the technological base is perfectly secure, everything around it can be built in such a way that security is the norm.

Cybersecurity today is unfortunately an area in which only those with a large budget can invest. In the 21st century, one of the major concerns regarding the protection of privacy was highlighted by the recent growth of the amount of personal information used and monetized by companies like Facebook. It is because of this, no one wants such data to be disclosed to third parties without their consent.

Why must the blockchain be adapted to cybersecurity?

Blockchain technology eliminates intermediaries and central authorities by promoting a fully distributed system. This point cannot be stressed enough. In the security of information systems, many applications rely on a "certification authority" (electronic signature, certificates, etc.). The latter is a guarantee of trust between third parties during exchanges (messaging, commerce, online statements, voting ...), in this context, blockchain could greatly change our environment. Within a structure (company or administration) the security of exchanges could be guaranteed by the establishment of a local chain (which also has the excellent idea of being auditable).

One of the recent developments of the blockchain lies in the notion of " **smart contracts** ".

Smart contracts are programs, accessible and auditable by all authorized parties, whose performance is monitored and verifiable; designed to execute the terms of a contract automatically when certain conditions are met. The rules governing the program may cover, for example, any verifiable event in a computerized manner.

We can therefore imagine a development to improve intrusion detection by implementing blockchain technology within a corporate network. The trust between machines would then be based on " smart contracts " which, when they are broken (machine compromised), trigger alert mechanisms.

In addition to intrusion detection within a trusted network "monitored" by a blockchain, the most trivial applications should emerge in the exchanges between connected systems. Here again, the dual interest of technology is based on the notion of decentralized trust and traceability two essential aspects for cybersecurity.

The Implementation of Blockchain in Cybersecurity

The developments in Blockchain have expanded well beyond accounting and cryptocurrency. The integration of intelligent contract development into Blockchain platforms has been introduced in a wide range of applications, including cybersecurity mechanisms.

Also, Blockchain's decentralized and distributed network ensures that companies avoid the existence of a single vulnerable point, which makes it difficult for malicious elements to try to steal or manipulate commercial data.

Blockchain transactions can be audited and tracked. In addition, at the time of execution, public Blockchains are based on a distributed network, thus eliminating the existence of a single control point. For attackers it is much more difficult to attack a large number of globally distributed pairs instead of having to attack a centralized data center or network environment.

Since a Blockchain system is protected with the help of accounting books and cryptographic keys, attacking and manipulating it is an extremely difficult task. Instead of proceeding to store them in a single network, Blockchain decentralizes the systems by distributing the accounting book data in several systems. This allows technology to focus on data collection instead of having to worry about the possibility of each data being subtracted. In this way, decentralization has allowed to improve the efficiency of the systems operated by Blockchain.

How does it work?

To be able to penetrate a Blockchain system, the attacker must enter each of the systems in the network to manipulate the data that is stored in the network. The number of systems stored in each network can amount to millions. Since domain editing rights are only granted to those who request them, the hacker will not get the right to edit and manipulate the data even after hacking a million systems. Since such manipulation of data in the network has never occurred in Blockchain, it is not a task that is easy for an attacker.

On the other hand, the hashing feature of the Blockchain technology is one of its underlying qualities that make it especially noteworthy.

Through the use of cryptography and the hashing algorithm, the Blockchain technology converts the data stored in our accounting books. This hash encrypts the data and stores it in a special language in such a way that said data can only be deciphered using keys stored in the systems. In addition to cybersecurity, Blockchain has many applications in various fields that help maintain and secure data. The fields in which this technology is already demonstrating its capabilities are finance, supply chain management and intelligent contracts with activated Blockchain.

When we store our data in a Blockchain system, the threat of a possible hack is eliminated. Each time our data is stored or inserted into accounting books, a new block is created. Subsequently, said block stores a key that is generated cryptographically. This key becomes the unlocking key for the next record that will be stored in the ledger. In this way, the security level of the data is extremely high.

Part 4
AI in Cybersecurity

Chapter 17
A Look Into How AI Is Used In Business Today

Put your fears to rest. Machines are not going to be our overloads. Yet. However, if we consider how they have entered the way we play, work, live and communicate, it will not be long before machines become a major aspect of daily life. Thanks to the businesses that have implemented artificially intelligent (AI) systems, this is partly true.

Automation is basically explained as enhancing process of decision-making. And with the rise of AI, machines and algorithms can uncover patterns to copy human action, thus automating business processes and freeing up resources to create extra business value. With AI, insights can be exposed for decision-making, and domain knowledge can be captured, shared and monetize both externally and internally. The automation of human interaction through AI is facilitated by digital platforms that produce metadata and domain data about how an organization is presently running its business. This data fuels insights and tasks carried out by the machines.

By 2020, according to statistics, about <u>40 percent of mobile interactions</u> are projected to actively request support from smart agents. It has also been <u>scientifically proven</u> that work performance can be improved by artificial intelligence. In fact, <u>75 percent of development teams</u> are expected to integrate AI functionality in services or applications.

To get a better concept of the implications of AI, we have to analyze businesses actively using it.

Produce important consumer insights with data

For many businesses, data has always been a valued item. For consumer services, this may be in form of customer information. For enterprises, this data may be in form of employee information. But before the rise of artificial intelligence and machine learning, this data was mostly unstructured which essentially made it difficult to derive anything valuable from it. Of course, a company might identify which products or services sells faster than the rest; however, the "why" stays unknown.

Simply put, before AI and machine earning, streams of marketing opportunities generally were wasted.

Nowadays, AI systems are not just facilitating consumer-based companies <u>improve data structuring</u>, but they are likewise making sense of it. Collected data helps them in connecting with customers quicker while improving customer engagement as well. Today, for instance, many businesses use AI to personalize shopping experiences. To implement a conversion of more visitors into buyers, brands are leveraging AI to obtain online customer preferences. AI tools, fused into brand websites, ask shoppers a series of questions in order to gain insight into their minds.

With AI, consumer trust can be gained. While some retailers may thrive on fake reviews, their success is usually short-lived, as products fall short of the online reviews. In cases like this, the brand image of such online stores is damaged.

To fight this act, Amazon, a merge ecommerce brand, is using AI to protect its image. Via an internal machine learning system, Amazon is pushing marked-as-useful verified customer reviews and purchase recommendations to the top of the page.

Make services more available

When it comes to calling customer services for enquiries, the frustration a customer feels when redirected or put on hold cannot be overemphasized. While hastening the purchase process is a step in the right direction, however, customers usually have several simultaneous queries or orders that can end up delaying the entire process.

For customers and business, factors such as long waiting time have often been an issue. Therefore, to make services more available, businesses have begun to invest in AI tools that meet this need.

These tools include chatbots, which are basically digital personal assistants with AI skills like NLP (Natural Language Processing) and machine learning. With chatbots, businesses are making their services more available by providing prompt customer service, using these virtual assistants. Alongside being readily available, these messenger bots knowledgeable due to their machine learning capabilities—which allow learning from interactions and retaining acquired knowledge.

Chatbots are capable of offering customer support, answering questions and providing sales suggestions.

Also because of chatbots, there are quicker services in the order line. Many buys would prefer to forgo that waiting line and order ahead. Today, some companies in the food industry are leveraging virtual AI assistants to help customers order food through voice command while waiting in line. Take for example the Starbucks' "My Starbucks Barista" feature.

The marketing potentials for AI are tremendous because it is responsible for creating a shopping preference for customers when you shop on Amazon, showing related or new items they may want. As AI-powered chatbots become more advanced and adopted in websites and social platforms, they will predictably become nearly as good as humans will in the future. Due to the speed and ease of chatbots, there is a substantial and instant impact on customer service and sales.

Even now, we have AI-driven content creating tools capable of performing tasks such as converting blog posts into social media posts and short videos. While these products may not be advanced AI, the potentials of these technologies, to improve business and marketing tasks, is thrilling.

Improve business processes

A healthy business values healthy competition. That is why they go all-out to get any factor that can give them winning-edge insights. Data is one of these factors. However, traditional computations were mostly ineffectual in identifying valuable patterns that might aid in refining business processes. This was so before artificial intelligence took over.

AI currently provides businesses the chance to <u>increase analytical capabilities</u> to obtain important insights from huge volumes of data in computer databases and online. It is very difficult for employers to monitor the productivity of workers during any particular time. Recently, some companies now use AI-powered digital assistants to carry out this task.

AI can also assist in reducing labor-intensive factors and processes such as human error which can result in ineffectiveness in work processes. Some firms are now even replacing their employees with AI systems capable of analyzing customer data.

From powering self-driving cars to answering consumer queries, AI is now becoming an essential aspect of everyday life. Businesses, of course, are not exempted, as private bodies and government are investing in AI—with the hopes that it will transform the future of employment and, eventually, the economy.

Living in an AI world

Technology is changing everything. It is changing our future. Self-driving cars and androids with human-like characteristics are now a thing. One driving force in this era of advanced technology is artificial intelligence. Artificial intelligence has revamped the way we do things, coming in form of smartphones, smart cars, personal assistants, video games, chatbots, and so on.

Thanks to the power of artificial intelligence, a digital computer is capable of performing tasks by simply observing the environment to improve its chance of success. While AI has made our lives much better, because it serves us personalized results that cater to our specific needs, this advanced tech is now on the threshold of prevailing over human intellect. Today there are computers that are able to find meaning, reason, learn from experience, and generalize like humans. The future is here. A future run by artificial intelligence that can successfully understand human speech through voice recognition, run autonomous vehicles, play strategic game systems, interpret complex data and even videos and images.

With rise of Watson, Alexa and Siri, it is hard to deny that we are living in an AI world. Artificial intelligence is capable of understanding context and concepts. From performing robotic surgery to telling the weather, the large processing capacity of AI is faster than the human mind in computational ability and is making headway in usually "human" regions such as inference and strategic thinking.

AI provides the chance for businesses to automate routine tasks, allowing humans to better utilize their time and provide greater value contributions. And from marketing to manufacturing to financial service, AI in business has grown into a vital, results-focused technology used in every function and industry. For instance, with talent acquisition and HR, AI is playing an important role in finding, managing and evaluating candidates for companies.

Just like the invention of the stream engine, printing press, machine-made clothing, internet and jet propulsion, AI is proving to become a transformative force in our society and businesses. Currently, AI in business is demonstrating its major influence on data-driven industries, because the technology lets professionals to make decisions that are more informed. For the sole reason of making informed decisions, companies like Microsoft, Facebook, and Google are powered by AI.

Other data-intensive outfits such as banks and credit card companies are in a comparable state. AI is carrying out tasks like assisting credit card companies in identifying sham transactions and blocking them—without allowing any case of false positives for valid customers attempting to use their cards.

From enhancing inventory management to behavioral targeting, AI can assist with anything business-related. AI features are starting to remove mindless and repetitive tasks. For businesses that are embracing AI, there is bound to be much more active competition as well as gains in productivity.

Robots are now working in warehouses and flipping burgers in fast food restaurants. Basic bookkeeping, investment portfolios, and insurance claims are now handled by artificial intelligence. AI is capable of performing basic HR tasks and doing legal research.

Improved cybersecurity

Also, when it come to the area of combating cybersecurity threats, AI in business is key. For people working in security operation centers, there is an array of functions to be implemented in the case of a security breach. They must detect intent, make out the intruder, estimate the impact, and defuse the attack before tangible impact happens. Seeing there are heaps of events like this on a daily basis, it is an unmanageable task without the assistance of AI, no matter the number of experts tackling the issue.

To prevent credit card fraud, AI can be help in monitoring and flagging activities related with fraud. In fact, such security platform is constantly self-adjusting so as to assimilate and learn from the data it is fed. Therefore, AI is immensely useful as an early-cautioning system.

AI 'will not' replace humans

With the growth of AI in recent years, there is one current discussion about how AI will affect the future of humanity, especially the job market. Experts are starting to weigh the pro and cons of an AI takeover. Should we welcome or fear it?

A theory about the "rise of robots" has predicted that advancement in technology will be ending almost 50 percent of industrial workforce worldwide. Many experts believe that if automation is not well planned and not tackled thoroughly, it might cause a major workforce disaster and affect more than 60 percent of current occupations. These jobs will either under marginalization or total elimination. Even in today's climate, automation threatens 69 percent of India's workforce and 77 percent of China's labor, according to a study by World Bank.

While the fear of AI replacing countless jobs is legitimate, we still need to understand that technology can also be reshaped to provide more jobs and business opportunities. Automation and digitization will, of course, allow for IT professionals who are knowledgeable in big data, cybersecurity, machine learning, cloud computing, etc.

Another school of thought embracing the AI takeover believes that automation will reduce the cost of production, improve the quality, quantity, and demand of goods produced in a short period of time, thus making more profit for the manufacturers who can then pay higher wages to their employees.

Ultimately, if automation takes jobs away, remember that its adoption will create other job openings as well. We must be ready to recover and adjust if we are very going to deal with the unavoidable AI future.

Of course, it is predestined that artificial intelligence will make some labor obsolete—as technological improvement has done in the past. But its effect, in the long run, will help the economy grow while developing new ways to keep people engaged. So if automation eliminates some jobs, it is capable of creating others. In America today, close to 30 percent of new jobs available now did not exist (or barely existed) 25 years ago, so to predict what kind of employment will be available in the next 25 years is simply presumptions. Some have guessed that artificial intelligence might create openings for AI supervisors, new system repairers and maintainers, cybersecurity experts and those who would reshape and improve existing infrastructure, e.g. self-driving cars. In all, it is hard using today's technology to products which jobs would pop up in the future.

Moreover, with AI in business, the future is looking very good. In spite of the worries of this happening, machines cannot totally replace human beings. It still does not have human judgment. Humans are still needed program the response of self-driving vehicles, say, a pedestrian crosses the road.

But while AI may take some jobs, it will create new ones with the data it provides. AI is meant to complement and enhance humans, allowing businesses to automate tasks so that humans can carry out other valuable business activities.

AI, automation and employment

Many automation optimists argue that throughout history technology advancement has never resulted in massive unemployment. It is believed that automation will allow factories save more money on labor. Therefore, they will either be able to lower the prices of their goods and services, thus improving the appeal and demand of their products. Increased demand means more profit and growth, so factories will expand and need more workers. With more profit, factories will pay higher wages. Buying power is increased, thus more consumption, or investment is increased due to higher income. Either case, production is increased, thus leading to a proportional rise in employment.

Amazon is a present-day example of this situation. Over the last couple of years, the company has effectively increased the thousands of working robots in its warehouses by 30 times. Yet during the same period of this robotic surge, Amazon's hiring rate remains the same.

The viewpoint of the automation optimist, in this case, is that Amazon is lowering prices thanks to its robots. Lowered prices mean more demand, thus meaning that the company requires more workers in its warehouses even though it requires fewer human hours of labor per packaging. Many optimists also think the fear of job loss due to robots is exaggerated because of the steady rise of ecommerce, especially when ecommerce is creating a demand for warehouse labor. Note that advancement in technology and increase in employment mostly have a positive relationship in manufacturing firms, across every sector, especially in companies with computer adoption.

Almost onequarter of the tasks assigned to a CEO can be automated. Machines will not completely steal our jobs but change the way we do them. The CEO, for instance, would no longer waste time analyzing reports if artificial intelligence can quickly draw a more efficient conclusion; he would then divert his time to other activities.

Automation would free us from routine tasks, expanding the business horizon to more interesting things. So when we stop doing redundant, obsolete work, our work rate for more important tasks becomes faster. Take for instance the case of a building maintenance company with a crew that uses drones to survey roofs for maintenance needs. Before the advent of drones, humans were climbing onto the roof for surveys. Now that the crew remains on the ground, safety is improved. The job of surveying roofs remains the same for the crew even after the robots have made the task easier.

Another example is the effect of automation on banking offices: zero job loss. Take, for instance, an automation software tasked with checking the balance of the customer's second account when he or she overdrew from the first. The software then transfers funds from the second account to the first to cover the debit. Because of the cost and tediousness, humans were never needed for this process; automation through this software will only make the customer experience better instead of making bankers obsolete. Take the case of another banking automation software that allows customers to close the account of their stolen credit card by imputing their details instead of speaking to a customer service representative. As automation drops on-hold time, the bank's customer service representatives can spend time on other tasks.

Chapter 18
The Difference between
Predictive Analytics and AI

The fact remains that the artificial intelligence (AI) industry is booming. It is already transforming industries worldwide, and companies are striving to integrate this developing technology. However, AI is not a new concept. The technology has been around for a while. But the only the difference we are experiencing now is how it has been leveraged in cloud-based services, computing and businesses. With the growth of AI, developers are now creating cutting-edge products tailored to a specific business need. Products that will deliver quick, practical, and significant results. But before any business can harness and execute its AI strategy, it must first know the difference between AI and predictive analytics.

Before we can explain predictive analytics, we need to talk about data analytics.

Data Analytics

Data analytics involve the processes of examining raw data so as to draw conclusions about the information they contain. In this case, several algorithms and statistical models are used to get insights to back decision-making. This technique is commonly used in commercial industries to assist organizations to make more accurate business decisions with solid support or evidence.

Many businesses today are familiar with data analytics. They can either benefit or probably suffer from the large amount of unstructured data they deal with. This data could range from CRM data analysis to user-tracking data on websites and apps.

To form patterns, data analytics is used to review data from past events. In this case, data is mined and analyzed to deliver commonalities, like percentages, ratios, and averages. By aggregating data to deliver a result, patterns and relationship between variables are found. With this database result, humans can make assumptions and make decisions concerning future events. Because data analysis is built around past events, it is descriptive and does not forecast the effect of an alteration in a variable.

This is where predictive analytics comes in.

Predictive analytics

Data analytics points logically to predictive analytics. In order to forecast what might occur or foretell the future, predictive analytics is used in making tests and assumptions about gathered data. Predictions are based on historical data and are dependent on human interaction, which is needed in querying data, validating patterns, creating and eventually testing assumptions.

Basically, Predictive analytics condenses large volumes of data into understandable and useful information. While data analytics is designed to obtain information from past events, predictive analytics tries to predict the future based. Predictive analytics answers questions like how precisely will the sales of a company be influenced by a 20 percent rise in advertising expenditure?" This question leads to "what-if" analyses and simulations which give the user more information.

Predictive analytics application runs on three central components:

1. Data: The efficiency of all predictive model powerfully hinges on the quality of the historical data it is processing.

2. Statistical modeling: Comprises of the several statistical techniques that range from simple to complex functions used for the find inference, insight and meaning.

3. Assumptions: The conclusions made from gathered and analyzed data typically assume the future will be following a pattern connected to the past.

Data analysis is vital to a business on its way to success, and predictive analytics goes a long way in enhancing business productivity in ways like fraud detection, market analysis, risk assessment, and marketing campaign optimization.

In the past decades, important marketing campaign resources were misused by businesses depending only on instincts to capture market niches. In the present day, numerous predictive analytic strategies assist businesses in identifying, engaging, and securing appropriate markets for their products and services, in order to drive better efficiency into marketing campaigns. With predictive analysis, e-commerce sites can use their visitors' usage pattern and search history to make product recommendations. When products are recommended based on particular consumer interests, these business increase sales opportunity.

By analyzing scenarios that are likely to happen, predictive analytics is all about asking: what could happen? Therefore, to predict the future, businesses use predictive analytics uses dataset to find past patterns in their marketing and sales. With this knowledge, they can determine future sales leads, analyze customer relationship records, and do much more.

AI: machine learning

Artificial intelligence (AI) is a subfield of computer science; its aim is to develop computers capable of doing things typically done by human and precisely things connected with people behaving intelligently. Machine learning is a system of computational learning built on most artificial intelligence applications. In machine learning, algorithms or systems enhance themselves via data experience, without depending on complete programming. Machine learning algorithms are extensive tools capable of implementing predictions while learning from loads of observations at the same time.

Machine learning is seen as a present-day improvement of predictive analytics. Proficient self-learning and pattern recognition are the pillars of machine learning models, which routinely change based on varying patterns so as to carry out the right actions.

Several businesses nowadays are dependent on machine learning to enhance client relationship and discover potential revenue prospects. With little or no dependence on humans, the application of machine learning algorithm makes for top-notch predictions, thus guiding real-time decision-making.

Another major importance of machine learning to a business is immediate employee satisfaction. For example, companies can do a comparison between wages and employee satisfaction. Rather than plotting a predictive satisfaction curve against wage figures for several employees, as predictive analytics would recommend, the algorithm integrates heaps of random unstructured data upon entry, and as data is added, the prediction results are affected to generate real-time accuracy and more useful predictions.

This machine learning algorithm uses automated recalibration and self-learning for predictions. For enhanced predictions, the data is constantly updated and increased. AI machine learning is an improvement on predictive analytics because it is a system that is capable of making assumptions, testing, and learning autonomously. AI is built on several technologies, and machine learning is one of the most vital systems used by client-tailored businesses. Thanks to machine learning, AI can make assumptions, reassess models, and reevaluate data, all without human involvement. This a major game changer. By testing and retesting data, AI predicts every likely customer-product match, at a capability and speed unattainable by humans.

Complex analysis can be carried out instantly with larger number of variables, permitting the system to quickly learn. This learning then delivers small-target insights that could not be accurately done by human analysts across the world. Results derived from AI's machine learning can intensely increase conversion rates, customer loyalty, and marketing.

Remember

AI machine learning and predictive analytics share a vital connection. While businesses must appreciate the differences between predictive analytics and machine learning, it is just as vital to understand the relationship between them. Essentially, machine learning is a branch of predictive analytics. In spite of having similar processes and goals, there are two core differences between them:

1. Machine learning is capable of working out predictions and recalibrating models automatically and in real-time after its design. On the other hand, predictive analytics performs explicitly on "cause" data and has to be updated with "change" data.

2. Contrasting machine learning, predictive analytics still depends on human experts in working out and testing the relationships between outcome and cause.

Chapter 19
Some Practical Future Ideas for AI

Research on artificial intelligence began in the 1950s. Early approaches ultimately stretched to their limits, and from the close of the 1980s, research moved into a period of inactivity named the "AI Winter." But in 2006, the field started a revival, as brain science research is imported to AI research. The process termed "deep learning" was created, and there were vivid progresses in technologies like voice recognition and image recognition and voice recognition, which AI was founded on.

Now with the advent of AI, today's products can be transformed into newer, more intelligent products. The effect of AI has sent a shock-wave of progress across several industries, even reviving old and stagnant ones. From virtual assistants on smartphones to smart TVS to cleaning robots, AI has already been incorporated in many products. Now the future is set for nursing robots, drones, and self-driving vehicles to be powered by AI. And in years to come, it is set to make our lifestyles more convenient and richer with devices capable of analyzing information and storing it in the cloud. Future AI devices will be of real assistance in everyday life, providing users more intelligent support. In the future, the intelligence of AI will rise speedily. Even today, computers are relatively capable of reproducing intuitive, conceptual, and even emotional abilities of humans—and in a few more years, it is possible that AI will exceed human abilities.

In the last decade, AI has dramatically changed our world. Even as we look around today. Our technological advancements seem like something out of sci-fi novels. Vehicles are driving themselves, voice recognition of smartphones, hands-free devices are toasting breads or turning off the, and airborne drones are flying the skies. As AI and machine learning continue to manifest, notable progress will sure me made over the next decade. From personal life to government to business, the numerous forthcoming applications will affect almost every part of our day-to-day lives—changing the way we interact with our environment forever.

So the question now is: what we currently do now that we could not perform a decade ago? What is the future looking like here? Although we cannot see the future, we make educated guesses.

1) Improved security

Drones are looking to be major game changer in the way we do things in the future. Just think of how a smartphone would be viewed if taken back to the nineties. That is how much impactful AI-powered drones will get in years to come. Drones will be capable of transporting things in complex spaces and over short distances, which is not quite yet feasible today. Whether it is delivering medical products, ordered packages or emergency response, these things will become quickly possible. One great feature of drones is the ability to fly. The concept of having some device regularly inspect spaces that are difficult to examine will make our society safer. In this future, a network of autonomous drones will soar everywhere, interact with us, and take care of things.

Drones will come with an urgency similar to smartphones, using them as readily as you wish to perform minor to complex tasks.

2) Create new services (and possibly social issues)

Artificial intelligence actually is the improvement of our capacity to problem solving and ideas generation. Come the next decade, we may reach an inflection point, after then we will experience improvement at an extraordinary rate. Robotics and AI will have been integrated into business processes and will be having a key influence on efficiency across several industries.

Totally new AI-based services and products will have formed new industrial and consumer. Simultaneously, AI will come with new challenges, possibly most significantly raising inequality and perhaps unemployment as monotonous, predictable kinds of jobs become automated. There will likewise be serious issues in areas such military application of AI, algorithmic bias, security and privacy. In a decade from now, a strong debate about these concerns will have probably come to the front position of our social and political discourse. Discovering ways to tackle these concerns on behalf of humanity will eventually become a major problem over the next ten years.

3) Empowering businesses

Existing consumer-focused applications of artificial intelligence and machine learning still seem stuck, downgraded to performing what humans can readily do or only what we trust them to do. Over the next decade, these trust fences will be lowered, and because of that, the dependency for AI-powered machines and algorithms will rise. For example, if you were planning a vacation to Italy, you would trust almost every recommendation your friend makes, even if they had only once been to Italy for a short vacation, simply because they stated so. Likewise, complex machine learning methods are been used to provide very personalized recommendations to users; however, algorithms do not always enjoy the trusting advantage a friend's get. To completely obtain user trust, AI has to grow in expectation and acceptance. And in the future, developers will be to use machine learning to create location-aware technology capable of pushing the limits of consumer-based applications. This will help marketers, analysts and developers better understand and interact with their users.

4) Advancement in healthcare

In the area of healthcare, there are several things machines can perform to assist the doctor. Of course, the doctor's guidance will still be needed in the near future, but most of the busy task assigned to doctors will be carried using AI. When it comes to the career of doctors, which can span up to 40 years, the number of patients they see during this time frame is quite limited. Many health practitioners are usually overworked and exhausted; it is a big problem. They also do not have to keep themselves abreast of the latest advancements, treatment techniques, and research in medications. This is where machines will play an extremely vital role in the future. AI can review a far larger set of patient data of treatments and treatment outcomes. Therefore, if machines are working around the clock, analyzing treatments, and diagnosis, doctors can easily improve interaction with their patients, while using AI to improve medical outcomes. That, in my mind, is super exciting.

AI medical systems will accurately and extensively complement the doctor's human instinct, thus becoming one of the biggest health-care revolutions in human history. The fact remains that the medical knowledge of human health is broad and complex, with even the human brain struggling to meaningfully contain it. Nevertheless, with AI, knowledge is limitless, and accurate life-saving decisions can be made with factual diagnostic data. A future where an all-AI health-care is more preferable to all all-human affair is quite near.

5) Enable sustainability

Artificial intelligence is going to affect every aspect of human life as wells almost every industry. On a larger scale, aspects such as environmental challenges, climate change, and sustainability are starting to become a major part of societal discourse as well progress into the 21st centuary. Even major issues like energy, urbanization, and population growth are need to be tackled. When it comes to proper city planning and urbanization, if the areas that can be used to amend the city density are well mapped, movements of residents within such city can well tracked more efficiently. With the rise of AI, private and government-owned bodies can use this sophisticated technology to bring about more meaning and purpose.

6) Blurring physical and digital lines

Artificial intelligence is set to further the areas of spatial computing. Imagine living in a world where your computer is not simply limited to a particular device—it follows you wherever you go. In such a world, computers will be reacting much more perceptively than they are currently doing now. We are already seeing this today with the growth of virtual reality, augmented reality and mixed reality. However, imagine a computer that it is so aware and intelligent it does not even need hardware to function. A 3D world where eye-controlled interactions, hand gestures and digital voice controls.

7) Improve human intelligence

As computational power continues to rise, artificial intelligence will experience major improvement. Large amount of data amassed will play a vital role in improving the body of human knowledge. When computational power and artificial intelligence are combined together, more intelligent predictions can made. Man would be able to solve century-old problems and figure out the answers to mathematical and statistical issues. Governments, businesses, and individuals will be able to deploy the AI system in maintaining a sense of equity, creativity, and civility—while improving productivity with respect to human cultural specificities, dignity, and diversity.

8) Cooking

Artificial intelligence is going to work out in the kitchen, since cooking essentially requires an understanding of in what manner an entry of ingredients can be joined together in different amounts and in different ways. Even today, AI-based cooking and meal-planning gadget like Hello Egg can assist you in finding and executing recipes more effortlessly as well as watch your cooking and eating habits to create healthier meal plans. While there has not been much success in getting AI to cook your food, the next years promises a lot.

9) Better shopping

Amazon is pushing the limits, throwing a lot of money into research in order to simplify the physical shopping experience even more than the online experience, using advanced AI technology. While online-based spending algorithms are common today, improvements are still being worked on. In the near future, predictions will play a vital role as AI suggests the perfect products to shoppers, even making sure that the product is available at the storeroom.

10) Easier and secured payments

As artificial intelligence continues to advance, developers are working on a payment system where people can just pay for things by showing their face, thus saving time incredibly. In the coming years, innovative AI face recognitions algorithms will be inexpensive and quick enough to sustain daily transactions, as machine learning teaches computers to identify more faces. Apart from the facial recognition, developers are working on an innovative "biometric" analysis (based on user's voice) to allow for more secure financial transactions.

11) AI boss

In years to come, most CEOs could simply be replaced by robots. If we define management as the practice of detecting and appropriately allocating talent, then an AI system might just be right for the job. In fact, managers might get redundant in the future, as employees are so proficient in organizing by themselves.

12) Tailored dating

Even the romance scene will not be excluded from the AI takeover, making dating easier for all, thanks to smart algorithms. The concept is that AI gets to understand you so well that it can basically perform the Tinder swipes for you. With an AI-powered dating app, a notification just pops up and says: "There is someone across the road you might be fascinated with. He is also interested in you. He is free tomorrow evening. We understand that you both adore the same artist, and she is performing—would you want me to get you tickets?" In addition,

AI is currently helping people practice how to land dates, mimicking human interaction. AI chatbots are helping people interact with the opposite gender better. Moreover, with more future advancements, people will not be able to tell the difference.

13) Cyber-relationships

Like it or not, the sex-doll market is booming. And with AI-powered sex dolls being in the works, this future is closer than ever. These robots able to learn from their owners as well as evolve to form an "actual" relationship. While this might look as if we are just fulfilling the fantasy of sex-obsessed men, cyber-romance is always bound to get more realistic.

14) Keeping a pet

Although AI will not substitute the feeling of raising a child in the near future, the same cannot be said for pets. Many people depend on the soothing presence of their loyal furry friends on a daily basis—and what if your pet comes in the form of an AI companion capable of playing relaxing music or answering questions? Even today, household robots are getting cuter, more vulnerable and more lovable, as their "brains" are beginning to be capable of imitating a number of the most central features of a pet's intelligence. Apart from just being loyal, soon AI pets will be capable of growing up with owners and forming lasting connections as its persona continues to evolve.

15) Make, criticize, and discover music

While the Pandora service is capable of breaking down songs, analyzing them to make future recommendations, the AI future promises greater things for music lovers. AI music curators will no longer depend on the active feedback of listeners on records to form its own human-like music. Songs will be synthesized through AI, giving rise to a new class of AI artists.

16) Smarter betting (for bookies)

For bookies, AI could change the game for players in this sector. It is one thing to bar casino card counting (whether using an AI neural net or a human brain) but somewhat another to curb bets that are remotely done. How will unaided humans overcome the odds, in a system where an AI analyst can easily analyze every shot a soccer player has ever missed (or made)? Based on its data or combined expert predictions, AI can make its own unique projections. Whichever way, it is uncertain the extent of the winning chance a human competitor will have in the future.

17) Self-driving cars

With self-driving cars, short-distance plane trips may become a thing of the past. The day-to-day commute to workplaces will be easier, changing the game for mid-range trips and even creating a new type of mobile workers. By significantly reducing the amount of time spent on the road, self-driving cars will give drivers more productivity as they spend that compulsory 30-minute in traffic reading a novel or even working in their cars.

18) Real-time scheduling

AI assistants such as Google Assistant and Siri have tried at least to assist users in scheduling their numerous appointments. However, it is only recently that the advancement of artificial intelligence has allowed these virtual assistants to perform more than recalling previous appointments and repeating them. Nowadays, and in particularly in years to come, AI will be reading and understanding your conversations to create scheduling information in real time. If you and a friend agree to meet for coffee next Friday via chats or phone calls, machine learning algorithms could analyze these references to create actual meaning and recommend a scheduled point at your desired time.

19) Help with homework

Even in recent years, developers have created AI capable of performing as good as most humans on a standard mathematics test. This shows that AI is now capable of reading and understanding the questions autonomously, even diagrams. This means that, in the near future, AI will be solving problems as well as solving them.

20) Strategizing sports

Before now, the strategy of multiplayer team sports was too intricate for artificial intelligence. But currently, even with the almost limitless unpredictability of human ingenuity and behavior on the rink and field, it seems that AI could soon create brand-new strategies for the most studied sports in the world. Many sports games will be efficiently simplified and learned, in its simple principles, by a machine learning algorithm.

21) Improved financial services

There is a fear that bankers will soon fall into unemployment because of automation in the financial services. If artificial intelligence can provide improved financial assistance, the banking industry will see a major revolution.

22) Automated legal advice

Since laws are thought to be entirely perfunctory, a mechanical attorney is not something that is far-fetched. The truth is that quality lawyering is only possible when the lawyer can successfully work with (or work around) the law. With an AI-based attorney in the near future, our society will experience some change, at a fundamental and deep level, by offering a fair defense to people unable to afford decent human representation. Even today, in several places, the public defense corps is a total disaster — but artificial intelligence will not get exhausted, or worn-out, or become judgmental. AI-powered attorneys will able capable of providing sufficient legal defense to millions of people around the world in years to come

Chapter 20
AI's Role in Cybersecurity

How artificial intelligence is a game changer

Experts today understand that cybersecurity is changing—and artificial intelligence (AI) will be the shifting factor. But when we assess the existing risk setting, we will see that things have actively been changing before AI played a vital role. Way before cyber attackers started using AI, they organized intricate, multi-dimensional attacks to exploit the mass of new business vulnerability points unlocked by IoT, Mobile, and Cloud. A number of recent attack campaigns now use a blend of the nine attack routes—data exfiltration, transaction fraud, account takeover, malicious insider activity, run-time app exploit, lateral movement, social engineering, encrypted attacks, and advanced malware—to overflow defenders with intricate, puzzling threat data. While most cyber attackers may not use artificial intelligence to alter the course of cybersecurity, they will definitely use AI to raise the rate of their current attacks through automation, so as to intensify a new, database landscape of attacks that are already in motion. But, as the modern-day emerges, cyber-defenders would surely uphold the area of cybersecurity by setting up their own AI to put up a fight.

Therefore, if attackers can utilize AI, the defenders can as well harness the precision, speed and power of AI to actively manage our present-day's evolving threat situation. By deploying their own AI-based defenses as a standard level within their services, cybersecurity providers can stay ahead of the game. AI will help cybersecurity teams in numerous layers of defense: they will be collecting and analyzing security data from several data sources, tracking different threats, triaging huge alerts (thus prioritize reaction), and automating response systems. Once there is a breach, AI-based systems will be offering intelligent recommendations for speedy control while providing thorough forensics. When there AI deployment is done well, artificial intelligence will be able to offer better detection and quicker response—significantly improving the area of cyber defense.

AI will definitely make major impacts in the cybersecurity landscape. These include:

Minimizing false positives

It will supplement rules-driven detection systems with the machine learning systems of data visualization, association rules, pattern matching, and clustering. By utilizing these systems, AI will be swiftly filtering out and presenting the most important alerts to help human analysts in making additional investigation while decreasing both false negatives and false positives within an enlarged torrent of alerts.

Triaging

Artificial intelligence will constantly scrutinize through all system data in quest of unusual behavior, recurring patterns, and other outliers to present to the human threat trackers for additional investigation. Security information and event management (SIEM) will be used AI in analyzing packets, DNS, proxy, netflow, and network data. User behavior analytics packages will be applying machine learning on user data. To discover advanced, endpoint threat analytics (EDR) services will do likewise with endpoint data malware. And utilizing RASP agents, AI will be spotting application fraud and attacks.

Threat tracking

Whenever there is an attack, artificial intelligence will gradually respond to who was patient zero (where the attack came from), what occurred to the asset (the impact of the attack), what were identity of the attackers, what were the earlier chain in the attack sequence on the asset, and what was the reach of the attack (this includes what other assets were affected by the attack).

AI will be capable of mining past security logs, network and asset information, alerts and other important data to find patterns, associations, and clusters, presenting them to human trackers in a succinct way.

Incident investigation/analysis

Artificial intelligence will be capable of automating the assortment of machine-readable external threat intel data, and increasing the reliability and precision of this data for each company's exact setting. AI will likewise be capable of collecting and applying natural language processing and text analytics to human-readable data with appropriate threat information—these include the dark web, social media, forums, and blogs—to narrow-down the everyday research task of the human threat analysts

Anticipate threat

Artificial intelligence methods like case-driven reasoning and knowledge engineering will be used in creating systems which show an incident responder the action to be taken when there is an incident. AI will be capable of reviewing past incidents and codifying knowledge from specialists, while constantly modifying or creating new divisions in the major system as it studies and learns from new incidents.

Limitations to AI-Driven Cybersecurity

AI is certain to improve several aspects of cybersecurity. But for AI to actually deliver, cyber defenders will have to leverage AI systems further than the existing unverified learning methods utilized in threat analytics. In years to comes, it is safe to say that AI will become a major game changer in several areas of cybersecurity. However, when it comes to the next-generation cyber protection, the AI will have now will not be enough. Artificial intelligence—in its existing form, and even within the coming years—still has its limits.

Responding to incidents

Although a majority of cybersecurity professionals and companies are starting to see the importance of layering AI into their security framework, many issues still have to be faced before this modern technology can be adopted. The most significant issue to tackle will concern the vague usage of the term "AI" which frequently leads companies into feeling this technology can resolve every of their security issues by itself, when the fact is that it is only a single fragment of a complete security solution. Companies will have to understand that they cannot just use a run-of-the-mill AI solution and see their security challenges as resolved. Organizations will have to understand that to deploy and tune AI models takes substantial difficulty. They will have to capitalize on an AI-based platform which is run by capable data scientists and security teams. As security models and AI platforms continue to grow, cybersecurity may reach unprecedented heights.

For companies that want to involve operative AI to their defense in a cost-effective way, they will have to collaborate with a recognized managed detection and response (MDR) security firm deploying its own cybersecurity professionals and AI-based systems. In addition, organizations will have to bear in mind that putting out an AI-driven platform does not remove the importance of capable human cyber-security professionals. Organizations will still need capable human cybersecurity professionals to make certain their AI platform is asking the correct questions within their data, and eventually making decisions based on the responses the AI delivers.

In reality, over the next decade, AI will essentially create a need for more cybersecurity experts. As companies are deploying more AI-driven platforms to evaluate greater amounts of data for a greater amount of threats, companies will also need more human cyberse-curity professionals to analyze the output of these AI algorithms, to analyze risks, judge alerts, and respond with a selected path of action. Companies should continually consider the expansion of IT systems, networks, users, and data in every company.

Companies will face more alerts and more threats than ever. In addition, companies will need more experienced cybersecurity team in investigating, hunting, and responding to these heightened incidents.

Presently, the business world is facing a scarcity of cybersecurity experts. Sadly, AI will not be resolving this challenge anytime soon, but perhaps it may make this scarcity even more austere, further demanding a collaboration with recognized, fully-equipped AI-based MDR providers, rather than trying to create complete next-generation security proficiencies on the inside.

For many companies looking to transition into AI-driven cyber defense, an upgrade is very essential. Many still depend on managed security service provider (MSSP), or their own internally formed information security operations center (ISOC). They are yet to adopt a proper managed detection and response MDR service, not to talk of established, end-to-end AI competencies. However, as continues continue to suffer threats from AI-based cyberattacks, artificial intelligence will take its place as a standard layer of active protection in their security system. As more companies and industries embrace digitization, this unlocking additional vulnerability points and generating chances for progressively intricate multi-channel attacks, the need for AI in cybersecurity will rise significantly

In bringing AI to cybersecurity, companies must be sure of whom they partner with, because numerous MSSPs are deploying the bare-minimum level of AI-integration—just for face value. There is a substantial difference between a last-generation security provider trying to layer in next-generation security platforms and a provider with exclusive AI platform for MDR services.

The future is now

Nowadays, billions are being invested by corporations and nations to perfect AI, whose current growth has even surprised field experts. The gizmos and gadgets we experience in sci-fi novels and moves are becoming a reality. AI is now being leveraged by head fund bodies to maneuver the stock market. Google is now using this technology to speedily and correctly detect heart diseases. With companies like American Express utilizing AI bots to function as online customer support. Researchers are spreading their definition of AI, with different AI working on specialized intricate tasks, even beating their human makers in efficiency and performance.

In the last decade, machine learning has changed the game for programming. Algorithms, working independently without human programmers, are teaching themselves on immense data sets and generating the most outstanding results.

AIs—one built by Microsoft and the other by Chinese organization Alibaba—are now beating human competitors in a reading comprehension test. Algorithms are reading passages and answering a sequence of questions about them even better than humans do. Some supposed "narrow" AIs are around is, implanted in our Amazon recommendation and GPS systems. However, the main aim of AI is artificial general intelligence: a self-training system capable of outperforming human beings across a broad array of disciplines. The so-called AI "takeoff," aka singularity, will probably reach human intelligence and surpass it, in years to come.

When that takeover comes, simple AI will take millions of jobs—from factory workers to drivers to even insurance workers. On the bright side, with cheaper labor, the government will be able to pay every unemployed citizen a general basic income, liberating them to chase their dreams, since relieved of the must to work for a living. In another possibility, the AI takeover will massively result in failed nations, disorder, and huge wealth gaps worldwide. Still, many believe AI will change the world: with AI robots caring for the sick and the elderly, reminding them to take their medications or tracking down their eyeglasses. An AI "scientist" will be capable of unraveling the dark matter puzzle. AI-powered spacecraft will venture past the asteroid belts, colonizing and transforming the whole cosmos. AI technology will control and fight climate change by maybe transferring a large swarm of drones to redirect sunlight away from the seas.

Imagine AI helping with every area of our lives. AI helping people find dates, picking the most romantic/appropriate restaurant based on information drawn from the data of both parties. AI will be storing and remembering every conversation we ever had, every idea we ever scribbled down, even business meeting we ever attended. With this technology understanding you so intimately that it knows it everything about you and serves you what you want.

Imagine better and cheaper healthcare as a result of AI advancements. AI systems capable of working on the clock to keep us fit. AI-based home sensors always testing our breaths for early signs of melanoma, and nanobot swimming through our bloodstreams, fighting the viruses and bacteria, breaking up blood clots and flushing out toxins. AI-powered, on-call medical assistant monitoring our immune systems, metabolites, and proteins, creating a wide-range idea of our health so that doctors can know exactly what is taking place in our bodies. When we are sick, doctors will be to able track and match that illness with millions of cases as far back as centuries ago. Imagine AI being capable of reading neural signals as they go into the brain, fixing the nerve pathways to help paraplegics in finding mobility. Imagine AI revolutionizing the modification of our genomes, editing human DNA, taking off substandard segments, swapping them with stronger, advantageous genes. This eliminating sickness and any human deformity forever.

Imagine the prevalence of surveillance drones to help the police fight crime and prevent unrest. "Psych drones" to prevent suicidal jumpers along bridges.

AI no doubt is the future. What is left now is for everyone to get on board.

The Various Cybersecurity Risks AI Produces

Introducing AI capabilities

The objective of the field of artificial intelligence is the automation of a wide array of tasks—AI can be made to classify images, guide vehicles, play games, and more. In essence, however, AI could alter the way we do millions of tasks. But fundamentally, any task that human beings or animals utilize their intelligence to do can always be improved upon.

Although the field of AI was born in the 1950s, many decades of investment has brought about better results. Researchers have real-ized unexpected improvements in performance due to factors like stretched-out commercial investments, greater and more generally accessible datasets, growth of stock software frameworks for quicker replication and repetition of experiments, enhanced machine learn-ing algorithms (particularly in the field of deep neural networks), and the exponential progression of computing power,

With image recognition, for instance, AI performance has surged over the decades to almost a near-seamless categorization accuracy of 98%, even surpassing the human benchmark of 95% accuracy. Also with the case of image generation, AI systems can now generate synthetic images which cannot almost be distinguished from photo-graphs, although some few years ago the imageries they generated were unpolished and evidently unrealistic.

In the area of competitive games, from Atari to chess, AI systems are doing extraordinary feats. With the most difficult and puzzling games, AI systems can ingeniously explore for effective lasting strategies, learn from the game reward routes, and learn from man-made demonstrations.

From a security viewpoint, for example, the ability to use facial recognition in recognizing the face of a target and space navigation can be used in autonomous weapon systems. Likewise, the ability to produce synthetic audio, text, and images can be deployed for online impersonation as well as swaying public opinion through the distribution of AI-produced content via social network routes.

AI systems will likely become more effective at an even extensive assortment of security-based tasks. In addition, we should not be expecting to see a massive short-term advancement on any specific task. Over the past decades, several AI research fields, with the inclusion of robotics, have not experienced any massive breakthrough.

But in the long-term of AI, the prospects are great. While AI systems today are performing efficiently on a relatively small percentage of tasks that humans can do, in the future, however, we will see a steady increase in that percentage. Additionally, once AI has gotten to human-level performance, it is bound to surpass even the world's best experts in years to come.

When this transition occurs, AI systems will be playing a crucial role in several security challenges—to the point of outperforming humans.

Introducing threats

In recent years, artificial intelligence and machine learning have grown increasingly, and their advancement has brought about an array of useful applications. For instance, AI is an important aspect of wide-ranging technologies like search engines, spam filters, machine translation, and automatic speech recognition. More favorable technologies that are presently being researched or undertaking modest pilots are self-driving vehicles, AI-powered drones for advancing disaster or accident relief operations, and digital assistants for doctors and nurses. In many years to come, modern AI is likely to lower the need for human labor, massively advance scientific breakthrough, and improve the level of governance.

While these applications are promising, we cannot turn our backs against the possible malicious use of artificial intelligence. AI and machine learning has altered the security risk landscape for states, organizations, and citizen, AI, when used maliciously, could become a threat for digital security (as attackers train machines to socially engineer or hack victims at normal or super performance levels), physical security (with terrorists performing consumer drone hacking and weaponizing), and political security (done via through targeted and automated propaganda campaigns, repression, profiling, removal of privacy through surveillance).

The malicious deployment of AI will affect the way we are constructing and managing our digital structure and also how we are designing and distributing AI systems, thus we will probably be needing policy as well as other official reactions.

It is important we ask ourselves: how can we predict, avoid, and (if needed) stop the dangerous application of AI? This question spans from the field of cybersecurity to counterterrorism, lethal autonomous weapon system, drones, and AI safety.

Security-based characteristics of AI

1. **AI technology works in two broad paths:** The application of artificial intelligence, like any tool or technology, can both be

positive and negative. AI systems, as well as the understanding of how to build them, can be directed both military and civilian uses, and more widely, toward good and bad objectives. And because some tasks that demand intelligence are harmless while others are dangerous, AI works in two broad paths just like human intelligence: harmful and beneficial. In reality, it might not be possible for AI researchers to just evade designing systems and research that can be leveraged for malicious purposes, however, in special cases, caution is needed in some particular research. Several tasks that would benefit from automation can also in function in two paths. For instance, systems that diagnose for weakness have both defensive and offensive applications, and the variance between the proficiencies of an autonomous drone delivering medical supplies and the proficiencies of an autonomous drone delivering bombs will not be quite much. Additionally, basic research whose aim is to advance our knowledge of artificial intelligence, its proficiencies and our level of control over its, seems to also fundamentally work in two paths as well.

2. **Efficiency and scalability of AI systems**: AI is said to be "efficient" when, after training and deployment, can accomplish a particular task quicker and cheaper than a man could. In addition, AI is said to be "scalable" when, after the completion of a particular task, it can increase the computing power it has accessed or make replicas of the system in order, thus being capable of completing several more kinds of that task. For instance, a standard facial recognition system is both scalable and efficient. After it has been designed and trained, its application can span several camera feeds—moreover, it is more cost effective when compared to a human expert doing the same task.

3. **AI systems outperforming humans**: An AI system can be equipped to outperform humans in any task. For instance, AI models can now significantly do better than the best players at games such as chess and Atari can. For every other task, whether harmless or potentially dangerous, there seems to be no just reason why presently seen human-level efficiency is the peak level of efficiency attainable, even in areas where human performance has been steadily high over the years.

4. **AI systems will raise mental distance and anonymity**. Several tasks require interacting with other persons, monitoring or being monitored by them, making decisions which correspond to their behaviors, or being present with them in the flesh. When such tasks follow automation, AI systems would be granting parties (who would have been doing these tasks) anonymity and better level of mental distance from the individuals they affect. For instance, an assassin deploying an autonomous weapons system to kill, instead of using a rifle, evades both the requisite to be at the scene and see the victim physically.

5. **AI developments are becoming a commodity**. Although it might be too expensive for hackers to get or replicate the hardware connected with AI systems, like drones or powerful computers, it is actually simpler to obtain access to software and important scientific breakthroughs. Therefore, within days, these sought-out AI algorithms can be replicated by any prudent hacker snooping the internet for new research. Additionally, AI research has a free culture where openness is paramount—as several research papers come with source code. Of course, limiting the spread of new AI developments will probably be hard to accomplish.

6. **Present-day AI systems are chockfull of unanswered**

vulnerabilities: Examples of these weaknesses include the exploitation of the design flaw in autonomous designs, antagonistic examples (inputs made so that they cannot be classified by a machine learning system), and attacks of fatal poisoning (bringing in training data which causes the learning system to make errors), and so on. These weaknesses are separate from traditional software susceptibilities (such as buffer overflows) and show that while artificial intelligence systems can surpass human efficiency in several ways, they can likewise be unsuccessful in conducts that humans never would.

Global effects for the AI threat

There are three broad far-reaching impacts of the threat of AI. Without the presence of an effective defense system, AI will be used to:

- Grow existing threats

- Present new threats

- Change the traditional nature of threats

Attacks will generally be more efficient, more specific, and harder to label, and probably exploit weaknesses in AI systems more greatly. This dramatic shift in AI application for malicious intents will definitely demand a response.

Grow existing threats

With all the several traditional attacks we have now, it is expected that advancement in AI will increase the number of people proficient enough to carry out attacks, the level at which these attacks are carried out, and the number of possible targets. All these are likely thanks to the scalability, efficiency, and the effortlessness spread of

AI systems. Especially, the spread of effective AI systems will raise the number of people capable of carrying out specific attacks. If the applicable AI systems are likewise scalable, persons already equipped with this AI-powered arsenal will carry out attacks at a much greater degree. Therefore, because of these possibilities, attackers would start targeting people they would not have otherwise attacked because of priority or cost-benefit reasons.

One clear instance of a threat like is the menace of spear phishing attacks. By using personalized messages to obtain cash or sensitive information from people, the attacker generally poses as one of the target's colleagues, family, or friends. The most sophisticated spear phishing attacks need a considerable amount of skilled labor, because the attacker must be capable of identifying appropriate top-value targets, researching the professional and social networks of these targets, and then generating messages which are credible in this context.

If a portion of the applicable synthesis and research can be auto-mated, then more people will be engaging in spear phishing. For instance, the attacker may not even have to speak a similar language as the target—as AI systems word the phishing messages in perfect sentences. Attackers may also be capable of engaging in large-scale spear phishing, in a way that is presently impossible, and consequently become more indiscriminate in picking targets. Comparable analysis can be carried on a variety of cyberattacks, and threats to political or physical security that presently and importantly needs human labor.

Advancement in AI may likewise growth current threat by raising the readiness of attackers to particularly perform some attacks. As mental distance and anonymity increase, this is very possible. If an attacker understands that an attack cannot be traced back to them, and if their empathy level toward the target lessens and thus they feel less strained because of their actions, they will be ready to perform more attacks. Mental distance is crucial, especially as demonstrated by the example of a military drone operator, who must still watch his targets and "press the kill button," often develops post-traumatic disorders due to his line of work. So, as mental distance increases, the psychology of the attacker is affected.

It should generally be noted that advancement in AI is not singularly the driving force of growing existing threats. Advancements in robotics and the cheapening of hardware (of both robots and computing power) are relevant as well. For instance, the spread of inexpensive hobbyist (consumer) drones, which can certainly be stocked with bombs, has now lately allowed terrorists to launch aerial attacks.

In the end, existing threats will worsen thanks to AI, which augments human expertise, intelligence, and labor needed to carry out such attacks. This shown in spear phishing and bot trolls attack, with AI delivering a multiplier impact to a malicious propaganda, making the attacking process quicker and easier, and broadening the number and type of plausible targets.

Present new threats

Advancement is artificial intelligence will allow for new breeds of attacks. These attacks may deploy AI systems to accomplish specific tasks more efficiently than humans could, or exploit the weaknesses of AI systems which are absent in humans.

First, because AI systems will exceed the capabilities of humans, attacks that seem impossible now will become plausible thanks to AI. For instance, not many people are skilled enough to convincingly mimic the voices of others or physically create audio files that sound like human speech recordings. But now there has been a dramatic advancement in the area of speech synthesis systems capable of learning to mimic the voices of others—this technology is even now commercial. As the output of this system become less indistinguishable from real recordings, without any particular planned authentication measure, mothers would not be able to tell the voices of children apart. A technology like this will be capable of opening up new ways of disseminating propaganda and imitating others.

Additionally, AI systems could be leveraged in controlling parts of the behavior of malware and robots which can never be manually controlled by humans. For instance, in a swarm of drones deployed in carrying out a physical attack, no group of human experts in the world could genuinely pick the flight path of each drone.

Also, in cases of cyberattacks, human control may seem impossible if there is no consistent communication channel once the breach is made. Simply put: a virus that is intended to change the behavior of an airtight computer, just like the "Stuxnet" software was used in disrupting the Iranian nuclear program, cannot get commands after infecting the computer. Limited communication issues can likewise be seen when a signal jammer is around or when the mission is underwater—two areas where self-driving vehicles can be leveraged.

Second, because of the presence of untreated weaknesses in AI, people who adopt modern AI systems will be opening themselves to attackers willing to particularly take advantage of these weaknesses. For instance, autonomous vehicles give attackers a chance of causing crashes by sending the cars antagonistic examples. A stop sign image with a few pixels altered in particular ways, which a human driver would quickly see as being a stop sign image, might still be misclassified as another thing by an artificial intelligence system.

If numerous robots are under the control of a singular AI system powered by a central server, or if numerous robots are under the control of duplicate AI systems, then a singular attack could likewise generate synchronized failures across the whole pack in an otherwise improbable level. A worst-case example of this might involve the attack of a centralized server used in directing autonomous weapon systems—this could result in a massive civilian target or friendly fire.

Finally, as technologies improve, new threats will emerge. Modern generative neural networks, used in producing realistic images and sounds, can be used by hackers to imitate realistic audiovisual signatures to sway public opinion, impersonate celebrities and politicians, design socially disruptive fake news, and unlock security systems. Malicious algorithms can be used in robotic or AI systems to disrupt, destroy, or control one or more capabilities or features of these systems.

Change the traditional nature of threats

The threat landscape will experience some changes as a result of both the growth of some existing threats and the rise of inexistent ones. The nature of threats will see some alterations as well, as AI-driven attacks become more efficient, highly specific, hard to label, and manipulative of weaknesses in AI systems.

First, the AI system's characteristics of surpassing human efforts, scalability, and efficiency will result in more regular and highly operative attacks (or with no considerable preventive measures to counter them). But before the weaponization of AI, attackers are often trading off between the scale and frequency of their attacks, on the one side, and their efficiency on the other. For instance, spear phishing is more efficient than common phishing, which does not deal with tailored messages to persons, but it is comparatively costly and cannot be executed at a large scale. The more common phishing attack manages to be lucrative in spite of the low rates of success simply because of their massive scale. If the scalability and frequency of specific attacks are improved, with the inclusion of spear phishing, AI systems can remove the need for any trade-off. This will help hackers because they will now be able to carry out more efficient attacks en masse with better frequency.

In addition, according to the scalability and efficiency characteristics of AI, particularly in the area of recognizing and investigating potential targets, highly specific attacks become more rampant. Attackers are usually interested in restricting their attacks to certain high-value targets, like rich people, celebrities, or political groups, thereby fine-tuning their attacks to suit their specific targets. Nonetheless, attackers still need to deal with the problem of trade-offs: trading between the scalability and efficiency of the attacks and how highly specific they are in this context.

AI will basically change the landscape of cyberattacks by raising the untraceability, precision, and efficiency of such attacks. A grim example of this could be the remote usage of drone swarms (autonomous weapon system) equipped with facial recognition systems to identify and terminate specific individuals in a crowd of people—with utmost precision.

Trends of AI in cybersecurity

Cyber attackers are always looking for new targets and fine-tuning the tools they use in breaking through cyberdefenses.

Massive data breaches

In 2017, the credit reporting agency Equifax experienced a cyber-attack that resulted in the cyber-theft of important information like Social Security numbers, date of births of almost 50 percent of Americans. This served as a vital reminder hackers are always working on a grand scheme—and no target (big or small) will be spared. These hackers are no going after organizations that house sensitive data, especially data brokers holding information about the person internet browsing habits of people. And because these companies follow little or no regulation, when one is breached, chaos is going to ensue.

Weaponized AI

While AI-based cybersecurity is taken shape recently, as researchers and security firms working with neural networks, machine learning models, along with other artificial intelligence technology to improve the anticipation of attacks and to detect the ongoing ones. It is now very possible that hackers will adopt similar technology in order to fight back. Sadly, AI provides hackers the necessary tools to achieve greet feats when it comes to security breaches.

Take spear phishing, for instance, that deploys a judiciously directed digital message to fool unsuspecting people into sharing sensitive data or installing malware. Machine learning model are now capable of matching humans by convincingly creating false messages, churning them out more and more without being exhausted. Hackers are now leveraging the autonomous nature of AI to deliver more phishing attacks. Likewise, AI will be used in the future to assist attackers in designing malware that is better at tricking security programs which attempt to identify bad code before it is entered in the system of organizations.

With computer programs training themselves, the sophistication and knowledge growth of machine learning can be scary when it falls into the wrong hands. These type of attacks, which look like sci-fi tropes, may take over the world in the next decade. Apart from the several benefits of this technology, such as better automation and computing with human assistance, AI-based attacks will be dangerous and hard to stop.

To hack and weaponize cars and drones

Researchers and technicians have warned about the dangers of an AI-driven cyberattack. For us to be on the safe side, it is very critical that we adopt practices that would keep our data and computer—from corporations to the government data—protected from attackers.

AI could be deployed in hacking into self-driving cars and drones, and turning them into possible weapons. *Waymo*, a Google-made self-driving car makes use of deep learning to maneuver real-world roadblocks; therefore, it is possible for AI-driven attacks to breach traditional anti-malware systems in the cyber landscape.

In 2017, according to a study by American cybersecurity providers Symantec, in a total of 20 countries, 978 million were victims of cybercrime, losing a total sum of $172 billion, thus averaging $142 per individual. The fear that artificial intelligence will result in a new age of breaches in the cyber landscape capable of bypassing traditional counterattacking methods. While AI-driven cyberattacks is relatively at its infancy, it will not be long before hackers use this technology to cause considerable network damages ad breaches without being detected.

IBM Deep Locker

As AI begins to grow in reach and usage, it is obvious that attackers will begin to start deploying it to their benefit—to the point of weaponizing it. That is why researchers at IBM created a technology called Deep Locker to fundamentally show how current open source AI systems can be combined with existing malware attacks to create a newer and more powerful kind of cyberattacks. Deep Locker deploys AI to hide its malevolent purpose in nonthreatening simple-looking applications, and only activates the malevolent actions once it touches a particular target (who hides information with an AI system) and then comes up with a key to choose when and by what means to crack open the malevolent actions.

The fact remains that this new breed of AI-driven attacks would bring about attacks that are more complex. When we compare these attacks to their traditional counterparts, we see that the difference is wide. These breed of attacks can be very specific, very evasive, and draw in a never-before-seen type of speed and scale of attack to the cybersecurity landscape. An attack that is cognitive and uses autonomous tactics and capable of working entirely self-sufficiently without the involvement of the attackers.

In addition, because of the adaptability feature of AI, it capable of learning and retraining on the go what was effective, what was not in the past, while breaching current defenses. For security providers to beat the threat of AI-powered attacks, they need to understand how they are being created as well as what their abilities are. A simple example can be taken from the medical field: when there is disease that is mutating (or evolving) again, like in the case of AI-driven cyberattacks, we need must then know what the bacteria is, what are the mutations, and where are its limitation and weak points so as to find a vaccine or a cure to it.

With the numerous forms of AI we have today, machine learning is a principally significant subsection of artificial intelligence at the present moment. Machine learning—a kind of AI—is used when applying intelligence to a particular problem. To know whether a process or file is malicious or not, machine learning can be deployed.

Malicious objectives

Sophisticated AI is becoming a mainstay of cyberattacks, now prevalent in places like China, Russia and some Eastern European nations. AI can be deployed in mining huge amount of social network and public domain data, thus extraction personal information such as email addresses, telephone numbers, location, gender to even birth dates, and much more. AI can be used to hack accounts as well as autonomously observe text messages and emails, also to design personalized phishing emails for social engineering scams, thereby obtaining sensitive information from unsuspicious users.

Artificial intelligence can be deployed in mutating ransomware and malware more effectively, and to find more perceptively and dredge up and take advantage of weaknesses in a system. Moreover, with the sophistication of artificial intelligence in the field of Deep Learning models to obtain better efficiency and accuracy, massive neural networks become have become accessible. The application of Deep Learning includes the areas of social network filtering, speech recognition, computer vision, and several other complex task, usually generating results better than human professionals do.

Also the accessibility of huge amounts of public and social network data sets (also as knows as Big Data) can play a vital role in cyberattacks. Tools of Deep Learning systems and modern machine learning are accessible today on open source platforms—this joined with the comparatively inexpensive computational structure efficiently permits cyberattacks with greater sophistication.

Nowadays, a large number of cyberattacks operate with automation. The human attacker rarely goes after a single target, as they are more likely to use the tools of machine learning and artificial intelligence in automating attacks—from malicious chatbots to ransomware, scripted Distributed Denial of Service (DDoS) attacks, and more.

Although we can argue that automation is basically unintelligent (on the other hand, we can also argue that some types of automation, principally those comprising big sets of intricate tasks, are indeed a form of intelligence), it is the notion of a machine intelligence organizing these automated tasks that is mostly distressing. An AI can generate intricate and increasingly directed scripts at a level and rate of advancement greater than any human attacker can.

The potential of AI is beyond our expectations—and criminals are looking to take advantage of this sophistication as well in targeting susceptible populations, performing quick-fire hacks, developing intelligent malware, and more. With the growth and maturity of AI as an everyday commodity, criminals will start improving the effectiveness of attacks, and also lowering costs at the same time.

AI cyber threat doubters

In one experiment to determine who was the most efficient agent (AI or human) in getting Twitter users to click on malicious links, artificial intelligence proved significantly better. The AI had to be taught to learn user behavior on social media and then create and execute its self-designed phishing bait. The AI-powered hacker was considerably better than its human counterpart was, as it was able to compose and distribute more phishing tweets than humans, and with a significantly higher conversion rate.

Bot or human? Artificial intelligence makes it hard to tell. Although this was simply an experiment, it shows that criminal hackers can work with AI and use it for malevolent purposes at a faster and more effective rate. This emerging technology poses a looming threat, but unfortunately, even when the dawn of AI is upon us, a large population of InfoSec experts does not want to accept the potential for artificial intelligence to be used as a weapon by attackers in the near future. It is baffling because a significant number of cybersecurity professions believe that machine intelligence is *currently* being adopted by attackers, and that hackers have improved in their sophistication in their usage of this growing technology—even greater than our expectations.

By weaponizing AI, hackers will be able to overcome their challenge of scale, as they try to attack as many individuals as possible, striking as many targets as they can, and in so doing reducing the risk to themselves. To achieve these feats, AI and especially machine learning are just the best tools. Tools which are capable of choosing when to attack, whom to attack, what to attack, etc.

Scales of intelligence and machine learning

As much as the weaponization of AI in cyber landscape sounds like a new concept, the truth is that it has been around for many years. And one weird thing about AI is that our notion of it has been changing over the years, and as our technologies more and more start to equal human intelligence in several vital ways. In the basic level, intelligence shows the ability of a body, whether it is mechanical or biological, to solve intricate problems. We have several tools capable of doing this, and we possess them for quite a while now, but soon we almost quickly disregard these tools once they because a part of our lives.

About a hundred years ago, for instance, the idea of a calculating machine capable of crunching numbers exponentially quicker than a human would have definitely been seen as a fundamental technological advancement, but not many people today will see a simple calculator as something great. Likewise, the ability to become a chess master was once seen as a top marker for human intelligence; however, in 1997, when grandmaster Garry Kasparov was defeated by Deep Blue, this cognitive skill has been stripped of its old glory. So with every transitory AI breakthrough, a newer definition will come to take its place.

Nowadays, quick advancements in machine learning (where systems are learning data and improving with experience without directly being programmed), neural networks (human brain-modeled systems), natural language processing, and several other areas are setting higher standards for what is defined as machine intelligence. In the coming years, autonomous vehicles, algorithms that diagnose diseases, and AI personal assistants (such as Alexa or Siri) will possibly and unduly lose their AI charm. We will begin to see these things as normal aspect of our live, and belittle these AI forms for not being completely human. Still, these modern systems of neural networks and machine intelligence are a form of AI will must not take for granted. To disparage the capabilities of these tools, we will be caught off guard by attackers who are willing to exploit the full potential of AI.

Another similar issue for doubters is that the notion AI invokes spaceage dreams and futuristic imaginations that can take one away from present realities. When most people think of AI, they think of Terminator-styled robots hunting down humans. However, that is not what artificial intelligence is. Rather, it is a wide-range topic of study based on the design of several types of intelligence which occur to be artificial.

Chapter 21
The Malicious Reach of AI

With the rise of the Internet of things, standard computing devices and wearables, artificial intelligence will unavoidably pervade every area of our world. But there are three major security landscapes we are most likely to experience attack, and in which the outcomes could be devastating. AI systems can be used maliciously in the areas

- Digital security

- Physical security

- Political security

Digital security

To create more efficient cyberattacks, attackers will use AI to automate such processes. As already established, these processes will include automated hacker, digital impersonation, and spear phishing. Within organizations, a new type of corporate subterfuge will be in the form of organized and antagonistic data poisoning, aiming to compromise, devalue, or collectively destroy the data structure of an organization.

- Digital security can be compromised when social engineering attacks are automated. The online information of the victim is used to mechanically produce tailored malicious links, emails, or websites they would plausibly click on, sent from addresses that impersonating real-life contacts, deploying their writing style to imitate these contacts. With the advances of AI, persuading chat-bots may prompt human trust by winning people over in longer conversations, and maybe ultimately masking itself visually as a known contact in a video chat.

- Likewise, weakness discovery will likely be automated. The existing forms of code weakness will be leveraged to hasten the finding of new weaknesses, as well as the design of code for taking advantage of them.

- To break digital security, more advanced automated hacking will be launched. Artificial intelligence is deployed (independently or with the participation of humans) to enhance the prioritization and selection of targets, escape detection, and resourcefully react to the alteration in the behavior of the target. For a while now, autonomous software has been capable of exploiting weaknesses in systems, however, more advanced AI hacking tools may show improved performance in contrast to the existing protocols.

- Convincing human-like denial-of-service will become rampant. Copying human-like behavior (via website navigation or human-speed click patterns), a large number of autonomous entities engulfs an online service, blocking the accessibility of genuine users and possibly attacking the security of the target system.

- Cybercriminals will leverage AI techniques in automating several tasks which consist of their attack channel: this could be dialogue with ransomware or payment processing.

- With machine learning, attackers will be able to prioritize targets for cyberattack. Massive datasets will be used to pinpoint victims more proficiently, e.g. by appraising net worth and inclination to pay due to online behavior.

- Attackers will be able to exploit the AI deployed in consumer applications, particularly in information security. Data poisoning attacks will be used covertly in maiming or creating backdoors for consumer machine learning systems.

- Hackers will be capable of remotely extracting the patented capabilities of AI systems through a black-box technique.

Physical security

As we while away productive hours with our digital devices, exploring the cyberspace, we still dwell in a physical world and occupy physical bodies. Even in that area, malicious AI is capable of catching up and posing dangerous problems. Apart from weaponized drones, life-threatening AI is capable of infecting self-driving cars, connecting appliances, and other devices, inflicting physical injury on persons and property.

- Terrorists can repurpose commercial artificial intelligence systems. In this case, commercial systems will be exploited in unintendedly dangerous ways, like deploying self-driving cars or drones to cause crashes or deliver bombs.

- Low-skilled people will now be endowed with top-notch attack capabilities. AI-powered automation of high-skill features—like autonomous sniper rifles (long-range and self-aim capabilities)—lower the needed know-how to carry out specific types of attack.

- The scale of attacks will increase significantly. As humans and machine team up through the usage of autonomous systems, the damage that persons or groups can execute will increase.

- Attacks will start to swarm. Dispersed networks of autonomous robotic systems, working together at machine swiftness, providing ever-present surveillance to observe large groups and areas and executing quick, synchronized attacks.

- No need for physical interactions. The attacker will be taken away from face-to-face interactions with the target or the environment due to the autonomous nature of the operation—with even the attacker not needing to commutate with the self-sustaining system.

Political Security

As shown in the 2016 USA elections, the deployment of technology—this includes artificial intelligence, social media bots, automation, and predictive analytics—can have a broad impact on the society. Particularly, AI can be used by malicious bodies for social manipulation, deception, propaganda, and illegal surveillance. AI-driven attacks can be used in analyzing human beliefs, moods, and behavior. In this case, these tools can help the goals of a dictatorial state as it appropriates AI in subverting democracy.

- States will use automated surveillance systems in suppressing opposition. State surveillance controls of countries will be enhanced by automated audio and image processing. There will also be a large-scale authorization of the gathering, processing, and manipulation of human intelligence for numerous objectives, like the clampdown on public dissent.

- There will be fake news reports with convincing made-up audios and videos. Very convincing videos will be made of political leaders appearing to make provocative commentaries they never really made.

- There will be a spread in automated, very tailored campaigns of disinformation. People in wing areas will be targeted with customized messages so as to sway their voting behavior.

- Campaigns will be influenced by automation. AI-powered analysis of social media is used in identifying major influencers, who can then be given (shady) offers or besieged with propaganda.

- Denial-of-information will likewise be attacked. Bot-powered, massive information-producing attacks will be used to overwhelm information pipelines with disturbances (in form of fake or simply confusing information), so as to make it hard to obtain actual information.

- Information availability will also be manipulated. Content gathering algorithms of media platforms will be deployed in driving toward or away from specific content so that user behavior would be manipulated.

Remember

The malicious uses of AI that would cause attacks on the availability, integrity, and confidentiality of digital systems (digital security threats); attacks on the physical world toward people or property (physical security threats); and attacks that result in the suppression of truths, spread of propaganda, and war on dissent in the society (political security threats) are not mutually exclusive. For instance, AI-powered hacking can be targeted at a cyber-physical system to inflict physical injury—with digital or physical attacks being executed to political reasons.

Chapter 22
How the Industry Is Trying
To Mitigate Cyber Risk

The range of cyber risks

Autonomous weaponized AI will do its malicious work surreptitiously and almost without leaving a trace. In years to come, it would be full-on machine against machine, as bodies try to protect themselves from AI-enabled threats. As we have learned, these AI-enabled attacks may not require an order from a base; they are capable of learning and making their own decision usually after breaching the target's defenses—learning fast from their environments.

As autonomous AIs become a mainstay of digital security, attackers can now leverage AI systems in infiltrating their target's system infrastructure as well as remaining undetected from many days to even years. By using their intelligence, these algorithmic entities are capable of blending in with day-to-day channels of network activity. Attackers will, of course, have a specific target and plan—to make money, cause mischief, or cause harm, as they hide in the networks of private and government bodies. The longer the attackers are able to infiltrate a system, the better and stronger they advance in their understanding of the network and its users—in time, they will be building up control over data and overall systems.

Similar to the HIV virus, which is so malign because it deploys the defenses of the body to duplicate itself, these new AI-enabled attacks will go after the particular defenses positioned against it. They will be able to comprehend the backbone of every firewall, the analytics systems deployed to identify attacks as well as "lax" periods of security in the target's framework. AI-enabled attacks will either be able to weaken, evade, or adapt to the firewall, even using its strength to disseminate, allowing channels for contamination and compromise devices with ruthless efficacy.

By impersonating others, cybersecurity will be at risk as well. As AI assistants, which help us schedule meetings, find restaurants, and serve as reminders, become more diffused, there is a growing threat when these virtual assistants become hacked. Or, actually, what would happen if weaponized AI were perfected to the point where it can mimic a real friend or family member you trust in the most convincing manner?

In fact, a surreptitious, enduring AI presence a network will have enough time to learn the target's writing style while sending an email, know contact base and the differences in personal and professional dealings of the target, basing it on the tone or language or themes deployed in the conversations.

With all these threats to our cybersecurity, and in spite of the increased investment in cybersecurity, organizations battling with major cybersecurity proficiency gap are usually made to believe that artificial intelligence, machine learning, analytics, and big data can save their important infrastructure and data from cybercriminals.

By analyzing the massive amount of data and aiding cybersecurity experts to recognize more threat than would have been manually plausible, organizations are taking up the fight against AI-enabled attacks. Unfortunately, thea same technologies used to advance corporate defenses can likewise be deployed in attacking them. As machine learning powers common internet scams like spear phishing by monitoring online behavior, profiles, videos, and shopping accounts. The more information that is available about a target, the easier it would be for an artificial intelligence to comprehend the target's habits and behaviors and take advantage of it so as to steal data or even the entire account. Cases of AI predicting the possible answers to security questions so as to reset passwords so as to take over accounts will become rampant.

Just like a human criminal, AI equipped with relevant information about a target could eventually fool that target into clicking on a malicious link or providing sensitive information. With the help of AI, attacks will be carried out more swiftly, effectively, and en masse.

As more targets become more possible thanks to the effectiveness of AI, more individuals and organizations will experience major data and cyber risks, with even public domain information undergoing exploitation. Although phishing for data is a basic but efficient type of attack, it is likely AI could be deployed by attackers to develop ransomware and malware smarter and quicker than any defense system or firewall the target can ever put up, by always changing the malicious code to evade detection or giving it more efficient means of attack.

AI vs. AI

So as artificial intelligence now part of the toolkit of a new-age hacker, defenders will have to develop innovative methods of protecting vulnerable systems. Gratefully, security experts have a rather obvious and strong countermeasure within their grasp, which is termed AI itself. The problem is that this is likely to generate an arms race between the contending parties: attackers and defenders. But this was ever going to be the case, because the only method of countering the other party is to ever more depend on intelligent systems.

For security professionals, this is Big Data issue—as we are talking about massive volumes of data—more than one human could feasibly generate. Once defenders start dealing with their attackers, they will no option but to weaponize AI themselves.

But to remain ahead of the game, cybersecurity firms should start conducting their own in-house research, and developing their own weaponized AI to test and fight their defenses. This tactic involves iron sharpening iron, so as to improve cybersecurity. The tactic is being adopted by Defense Advanced Research Projects Agency (DARPA—an advanced research wing in the Pentagon) when it organized its DARPA Cyber Grand Challenge, where AI developers pitted their AI designs against each other in an effort to "capture the flag." By exploiting weaknesses, protection will become a matter of the survival of the strongest AI—in the most Darwinian language. The aim of the contest was to improve the design of sophisticated, autonomous systems that detect, evaluate, and patch software weaknesses before attackers could have an opportunity to take advantage of them.

From countering cyberattacks to fraud detection, AI will play a very crucial role. As security firms have been practicing for years, AI systems deployed by defenders will be used in automatically detecting anomaly, knowing if a network has been compromised or attacked. By utilizing natural language processing to forecast upcoming threats, for instance, AI can automatically discover the timing and planning of an attack.

Machines can automatically discover and take advantage of new weaknesses very fast. Apart from closing down current security holes in the defender's system, the landscape of AI security systems will actively be programmed to counterattack, thus detecting vulnerability in the attacker's code and exploiting it before the holes are closed up. While this is a smart strategy for targets to defend themselves, malicious attackers could as well deploy similar techniques in counterattacking. Simply put: attackers might deploy AI for an attack just the same way defenders can use it for defense.

While attackers will continue to use the existing cyberattack methods today, AI will simply improve the effectiveness of those attacks. Therefore, AI-powered defense systems will also have to up their game to protect themselves against AI-powered attacks. But for defenders to truly stay ahead, there must be a continuous monitoring of hackers' cyberattack activities, learning from them, while innovating a blend of unsupervised and supervised learning defense techniques to identify and stop attacks before they spring up. At the end of the day, only superior strategies and defenses will overcome.

Humans becoming bystanders in the AI battle

Now as AI-enabled hacking becomes increasingly effective in targeting vulnerable systems and users, cybersecurity providers will also have to depend on artificial intelligence like never before. Sooner or later, these tools will go beyond human control and understanding, functioning at fast rates in a growing digital landscape. It will reach a stage where both defenders and attackers will have no option but to tap the "go" button on their own systems, and just hope for a good outcome. A feature of AI is that humans will be progressively taken out of the loop.

Cost-return decision

Although while AI and machine learning can be important tools for hackers and cybercriminals, they still need a massive amount of time and fund in designing them, to begin with. Even today, many people are still vulnerable to the most basic types of cyberattack. Across the world, people are still being tricked into clicking malicious links orchestrated by the most basic phishing campaigns. Even several high-level organizations are quite susceptible to breaches, with just one click of a button. There, why would attackers even worry about investing in modern methods when they are currently ahead of the game?

Why should attackers bother about developing a deep learning hacking system when they can just send 20,000 emails, the subject being around interesting subjects or juicy messages, hoping just one person clicks on them?

While cybersecurity experts value the importance of sophistication, however, there is no reason for brute-force attacker to care. Nevertheless, it is still conceivable that like any serious organization, attacking groups will be looking to take advantage of AI and machine learning tools to supplement their operations, if not replacing them with their manual tasks. In the end, hackers will be looking for processes to make their work smoother.

Protecting cybersecurity

- Lack of defense preparation and the direct deployment of modern and short-term AI to cyberattacks will result in a rise in the diversity, scale, and number of attacks.

- While AI-enabled defenses are also being technologically advanced and used in the cyber landscape, but more policy and technical innovations are required to make sure that AI's effect on digital systems is favorable in the long run.

- Cybersecurity is a landscape that will experience new and active usage of AI technologies, both for defense and offense. Even now, artificial intelligence is being used to detect malware and anomaly.

- Over the last decade, numerous vital IT systems have progressed and grown into massive entities, joining together several separate systems, undermanaged and, because of this, insecure. As modern cybersecurity is quite labor intensive but poorly staffed, AI automation can play a crucial role. However, the increased deployment of AI for cybersecurity may case new risks to arise.

- Lately, many attackers are actively carrying out advanced cyberoperations, such as highly specific cyberattacks. The cyber landscape consists of an intricate and massive arena of cybercrime, which often requires a high level of organization and professionalism. These criminal groups deploy ransomware, phishing, malware, DDoS, and other types of cyberoperations, and actively adopt new technologies.

Currently, artificial intelligence is being extensively deployed as a defensive cybersecurity measure, giving specific types of defenses, like malware and spam detection, more scalability and effectiveness. Simultaneously, several malicious parties will be motivated to deploy AI in performing experimental attacks on traditional insecure targets or systems. Their motivation may range from the inability to keep skilled labor on their side, labor costs, and speed of attack.

That is why researchers are trying to use AI for experimentally attacking purposes, in an effort to improve security while detecting weaknesses and proposing solutions. Nevertheless, the speed of AI advancements shows that attackers using machine learning systems to perform cyberattacks is going to happen—if it has not even occurred already. Motivated and sophisticated attackers are already augmenting their cyberattacks with AI, and in a few years to come, waves of AI-enabled attacks will become rampant

The US government body is actively invested in the blending of cybersecurity and artificial intelligence. Machine learning and AI are even seen as many as the future of cybersecurity. It is merely a matter of time before those two take their rightful space in the cyber arena. AI systems are currently intended to perform an extended role in US military operations and strategies, with the US Department of Defense already putting into place a strategy where machines and humans work together closely to meet military goals. Simultaneously, government is invested in foundational research in order to grown the scale of abilities of AI systems.

Certainly, over the next decade, the capabilities of AI cybersecurity will grow increasingly, particularly as new advancements in artificial intelligence (like in the field of deep reinforcement learning) are deployed in cybersecurity.

How AI is altering the cybersecurity threat landscape

One major future threat of cybersecurity and AI is that artificial intelligence might augment more massive scales of attacks, which are orchestrated by attackers with a certain level of resources and skills compared with the effect such attackers might at present be able to accomplish. Over the last years, we have discovered striking but disturbing piece of evidence of the notion that AI can be deployed for malicious applications in cyberspace. For instance, we have seen how a full autonomous spear phishing system can design customized tweets on social media network based on the shown interests of users, so as to achieve massive amounts of clicks to malicious links.

Massive attacks are becoming a phenomenon, with Russian hackers sending highly customized messages rigged with malware on social networks. If these attacks become AI-enabled (if they are not already are), imagine the scale of impacts they will have with automation. With modern natural language generation systems now available, AI systems could copy the way people write online and target their online communities with troubling, targeted precision.

In addition, attackers can exploit the automated feature of AI to discover the weaknesses of systems with less labor when compared with traditional hacking. Numerous organizations presently adopt security systems named Endpoint Detection and Response (EDR) platforms in countering more sophisticated threats. The EDR market is worth about $500 million in the cybersecurity arena. These tools are based on a blend of machine learning heuristic algorithms, offering capabilities like the prevention of advanced customized attacks and the provision of behavioral analytics and next-generation antivirus (NGAV). While these systems are relatively effective against tradition human-sanctioned malware, it is more likely that AI systems may be able to learn how to dodge them.

Attackers are more likely to use the growing capabilities of AI reinforcement learning, as well as deep reinforcement learning. Particularly, using the AI ability to learn from experience so as to design attacks that traditional IT experts and technical systems are not ready for.

Points of control and current countermeasures

Cyber risks are impossible to prevent completely but quite possible to control, and there are several points of control that can be worked on to improve security. As artificial intelligence and cybersecurity increasingly progress together in many years to come, a pre-emptive effort is required to be one step ahead of keen attackers. To control cybersecurity and mitigate cyber risks, here are several points of control, their current countermeasures, and limitations:

1. Aware consumer: If users become more aware of telling signs of specific attacks, like badly written phishing messages, and exercise enhanced security habits, like deploying two-factor authentication and complex and assorted passwords. In spite of the lasting awareness of the weakness of IT infrastructure, many end users of IT systems are still susceptible to even the most basic attacks—like how many unpatched systems are easily exploited. This is vital when it comes to the potentials of an AI-enabled cybersecurity landscape, particularly when the number of highly targeted attacks can be increased cover more targets.

2. Researcher and government: While AI is not directly mentioned in norms and law, several researcher norms and laws are connected to cybersecurity. For instance, the US Digital Millennium Act and the Computer Fraud and Abuse Act prohibit specific behaviors in cyberspace. Since legal enforcement is especially hard to cross

national boundaries, norms like the accountable revelation of weaknesses can help cyberdefenses by lowering the chance of a recently revealed weakness being used against a great number of targets before it can be patched. One relevant action that cyber-security researchers can take up is to detect weaknesses in code, giving security providers the chance of raising their products' security. Some ways to encourage this process is by:

- Paying for "Bug bounties," in which parties involved are rewarded for detecting and dutifully revealing weaknesses.

- "Fuzzing": an automated technique of weakness detection, in which several plausible permutation of program inputs are tried out—this is usually carried out by an organization's internal department to detect weaknesses.

- Products (at present obtainable) that depend on machine learning to forecast if source code may have a weakness.

3. Centralization of the industry: Spam filters are an established example of how the centralization of IT infrastructure helps defense systems. For instance, the effectiveness of Google's spam filter (as a result of its long-term deployment of massive amount of user data) has shielded many of its users from several basic spam attacks. In addition, several large networks are always looking for anomalies, thereby shielding its users from detected anomalies by removing them.

This is when economies of scale can play an important role—it is smarter to carry on reiterating a single spam filter for a massive number of users than to make each user design or install their own spam filler on their computer. Likewise, cloud computing firms may implement terms of agreement which prohibit their hardware from being deployed for malicious objectives, if they can detect such actions. Another method of system-grade defense is to blacklist IP addresses from the most common attacks originate from, although proficient hackers can hide the source of their attacks.

Economies of scale, as well as centralization, may also help in using AI-enabled defenses against cyberattacks, by permitting the gathering of expertise and labor and the collection of massive datasets for defensive purposes. Centralization is not a completely faultless concept because it is quite dangerous when the central systems are breached. Another limitation to this control point is that cyber attackers are capable of learning how to avoid system-grade defenses. For instance, they can buy commercially sold antivirus software and examine alterations between protection protocol updates to know what is and is not being secured against.

4. Incentives for attacker: Attackers can be stopped from performing attacks in the future or reprimanded for previous attacks. A required (but insufficient) condition of effectively preventing and reprimanding cyber attackers is the ability to detect the attack's source, an extremely problematic issue. A larger issue for people capable of attributing an attack's source is that even when they obtain topgrade information, they may refuse to share it, because of this may be compromising to their method or source. Lastly, some parties may not want to remand specific actions in order to sidestep making an example, therefore preserving the freedom to involve in such malicious cyber actions themselves.

5. Technical cyberdefenses: Vast arrays of cyberdefenses are accessible to many people today, although we still do not have a comprehensive analysis of their relative efficiency. While all the previously listed countermeasures are important, sophisticated

AI cybersecurity applications should always come first into play. Security firms offer a vast range of cybersecurity solutions, which range from threat detection, to programmed patching of their own software, to consulting services and incident response. Computer and network security products can help in preventing, detecting, and responding to threats. Features of provided solutions include the detection or prevention of attacker procedures, techniques, and tools, as well as the detection of software exploits. Major aspects of cyberdefenses include cloud security, internal network security, and computer security.

Machine learning models are now being gradually deployed for cyberdefense. This could be a type of supervised learning, where the objective is learning from established threats so as to generalize new threats. Alternatively, it could be a type of unsupervised learning, where an anomaly sensor notifies on suspicious changes from regular behavior. For instance, self-styled "next-generation" antivirus solutions usually use supervised learning methods in generalizing new malware types. Entity and user behavior tools can be used in monitoring standard application or user behavior, and detecting deviances from standard behavior so as to identify malicious behavior among a collective of variances. Lately, AI has been deployed by security experts in hunting for malicious attackers more effectively within their own organizations, by permitting interaction through automating queries and natural language to for comprehending likely threats.

Comparatively little consideration has been given to making AI-enabled defenses fortified against cyber attackers that expect their usage. Paradoxically, the deployment of machine learning for cyberdefense could really improve the scale and effectiveness of cyberattacks because this lack of consideration and other weaknesses.

Additionally, a larger proportion of cybersecurity experts nowadays still do not trust completely AI-enabled defense systems.

Recommendations for AI-enabled cybersecurity

An intervention is needed to mitigate risk caused by the malicious usage of artificial intelligence and machine learning. So, it is recommended for AI and machine learning policymakers, researchers, and other stakeholders to put these things into place.

- Policymakers should work together with technical researchers in investigating, preventing, and mitigating potential malicious deployment of artificial intelligence. Policymakers must be serious in preventing the execution of actions that will restrict or obstruct research advancements, except those actions will probably bring equal benefits. Joint collaboration with technical professionals will likewise ensure that policies will be based on the practical realities of available technologies.

- Engineers and researchers in AI should take the double-use (good and bad) capability of AI seriously. The appropriation concerns of AI should guide their research norms and priorities, and they must preemptively reach out to important parties when malicious applications are anticipatable. Since artificial intelligence is a double-use technology, researchers must be serious about doing whatever possible to advance helpful usages of the technology and avert detrimental usages. This could be working closely with policymakers and providing their expertise, especially in deliberating on the real-world potential applications of several research projects before concluding to execute it.

- Researchers should come together to identify research fields (like computer security) with more advanced techniques for tacking AI double-use issues and import them where they can be beneficial for artificial intelligence.

- More and more stakeholders and technology professional should come together to talk more about the challenges and solutions of cybersecurity. This could mean connecting with other sectors such as national security professionals, civil society, currently uninvolved cybersecurity and AI researchers, ethicists, organizations with AI-incorporated products, the general public, and several other stakeholders and important professionals.

Note that because of the double-use feature of artificial intelligence, several of its malicious usages are connected to legitimate usages. In some instances, the difference between illegitimate and legitimate deployment of artificial intelligence could be the intent of the user. For instance, surveillance systems can be deployed in catching criminals or oppressing common citizen. Information content filters can be used in burying fake news or spreading propaganda. Influential private bodies and governments will be able to use several of these artificial intelligence tools and could deploy them for public harm or good. This the reason why a public discussion on right usage of AI technology is vital.

These four recommendations will help facilitate cross-disciplinary discussion among policymakers, AI researchers, policymakers, and other important participants to make sure that AI technology is deployed to profit society.

Research recommendation for cybersecurity

As AI-enabled systems become more well-known and efficient, the likely effects of cybersecurity situations are increasing as well. As we have already established, artificial intelligence is vital to three major reasons:

- By increasing automation, there will be a rise in digital control of physical systems. Say, for instance, how much more control a skilled hacker could work upon a sophisticated car when than a regular vehicle built some decades ago.

- Successfully executed attacks on AI-enabled systems will grant the attacker access to the system's trained models or/and algorithms. Say, for instance, if the algorithm deployed for analyzing satellite imagery is compromised, or the dataset deployed for facial recognition on social media is stolen.

- When the use of AI in cyberattacks is increased, it is expected that the attacks become sophisticated and effective at a much massive scale. Therefore, the attack range will affect victims that would have likely been unsuitable targets before the involvement of AI.

To address these rising risks, cybersecurity must become a top and growing concern, so as to stop and control harms from reaching artificial intelligence systems. Likewise, the most effective cybersecurity practices must be imported into all the sectors where AI systems are applicable.

1) Learn with and from the cybersecurity community

Examples of ideas that could be worked upon by the community to improve cybersecurity include:

- Red teaming: A "red team" in cybersecurity is a group of security professionals or/and members of a host organization purposefully planning and executing against the practices and systems of the organization (with some restrictions to avoid permanent damage), with a noncompulsory "blue team" countering these attacks. To improve cybersecurity, a broad usage of red teams in finding and repairing potential security weaknesses and safety challenges should be a major concern for AI developers, particularly in important systems.

- Responsible disclosure of AI weaknesses: AI-based technologies should be designed in such a way that a trusted revelation of weaknesses found in AI systems (ranging from potentially antagonistic inputs, security weakness, and other forms of exploits) are revealed to users. When already warned of their vulnerability, users can proactively protect themselves.

- Predicting security-based capabilities: researchers should be to determine if "white-hat" efforts could be used to forecast how sophisticated AI will bring about efficient cyberattacks and more efficient cyber defenders.

- Security tools: researchers should ask themselves: what tools (if there are any) should be created and spread to assist in making it customary to test for regular security issues in AI systems—just like the tools deployed by computer security experts?

- Secure hardware: researchers should find out if security features can be added to AI-enabled hardware, for instance, to enable activity audit, limit access, stop copying, and so on. How practically and technically realistic is the creation and acceptance of hardware equipped with such features?

2) Explore diverse openness models

Nowadays, the culture of machine learning research community is very open. A huge portion of groundbreaking research is published online in papers that reveal things like source code, algorithmic details, and rough architectural outlines. This type of transparency is clearly beneficial to other researchers looking to advance the works of predecessors, collaborate, and join ideas together to create new ways of applications.

Nevertheless, transparency of AI technology can result in its misuse.

Malicious parties can easily access these newly shared algorithms and capabilities for nefarious purposes. This begs the question: it is right to refrain from simply postpone publishing of certain discoveries connected to artificial intelligence for cybersecurity reasons? Perhaps an example can be followed in the field of computer security, where finds that could impact vital systems are not shared publicly until the developers have gotten a chance to repair the weakness. When AI-related research findings are ever intentional withheld in our present times, it is often because of intellectual property (maybe to prevent a future finding being "jacked"). Although transparency is a good feature for any reputable research community, lowering openness has its own benefits as well.

In technical AI fields of special concern, pre-publication risk can be assessed. For some forms of AI research findings, like a discovery linked directly to antagonistic machine learning or digital security, they could be subjected to some type of risk assessment to see what level of transparency is suitable. For fields like computer security and biotechnology, this process is already normal.

To prevent "scooping" of AI findings for malicious uses, growing but commercial "central access" structures (where customers deploy services such as image recognition or sentiment analysis—generated by a central provider—without being able to access the system's technical information themselves) could become a platform where AI capabilities are securely shared and the chances of nefarious uses are significantly lowered.

In addition, sharing methods could be employed to facilitate security and safety. In this case, some specific types of research findings are carefully shared among a selected group of organizations and people that meet some specific requirements. These requirements may include devotion to proper ethical norms, effectiveness of information security, and so on. For instance, specific types of offensive cybersecurity discoveries that use artificial intelligence might be shared among trustworthy companies for weakness detection purposes, but would be dangerous if more extensively disseminated.

Finally, apart from artificial intelligence, researchers and relevant organizations will need to study the norms that have been applied to other double-use technology. The considerations, models, methodologies, and cautions that have risen while addressing parallel issues brought about by other double-use technologies must be comprehended.

3) Encouraging a culture of responsibility

AI-relevant organizations and researchers are well equipped to shape the security arena of the AI-powered cyberspace. This community should strongly make AI a social responsibility while encouraging others sectors and industries to do likewise. They should be able to use their knowledge while leveraging the experiences of experts from other technical fields—so as to address malicious risks together.

During the course of training, enlisting, research and growth, organizations and people should be aware of the dangers of malevolent usages of artificial intelligence capabilities. To foster a culture of responsibility, the steps may be followed:

- Education: What informal and formal ways of teaching engineers and scientists about the socially and ethical deployment of their technology are most efficient? This training could be embedded into the education of artificial intelligence researchers.

- Ethical standards and statements: Ethical standards and statements could be infused in AI research—enforced and implemented

- by a regulatory body. In addition, there would have to be a clear distinction between what is ethically harmful and harmless in the deployment of AI.

- Using whistleblowers: Whistleblowing protection and reward could be granted to people willing to out hidden cyber attackers.

4) Advancing policy and technological solutions

Apart from giving way to new cybersecurity threats and issues, artificial intelligence advances can as well likely create new forms of defenses and responses. These technological innovations must go together with and be sustained by well-crafted policies. Both technological and institutional approaches must be designed in preventing and mitigating likely appropriation of artificial intelligence technologies. To execute this, the following areas must be worked upon:

- Protection of privacy: Technical measures must be set aside to safeguard privacy from malicious entities in the AI landscape. Organizations, state or private corporations, should play a role in this regard.

- Organized deployment of AI to benefit public security: AI-enabled defense systems should be worked on to improve public security.

- Observing of AI-related resources. There should be a regular yet feasible monitoring of inputs to AI technologies like data, code, talent, and hardware.

Conclusion:
Fortify Your Data

Understanding these technologies is just the first step to truly protecting your data. As I look forward to the future of business, technology, and the world in general it is very clear to me that data is going to be the one of the most valuable resources. It is important to be mindful about how you store and use your data just as much as it is important to keep it safe.

As we move further and further into the digital age, I believe that cyber security will become simply 'security'. Just like any physical lock on a vault, any lock made by man can be broken by man. It is important to develop Blockchain, IoT devices, and artificial intelligence to become proactive instead of reactive to cybercriminal threats.

I hope you found this book to be a source of clarity to what data really is, how to protect it, and a base level understanding of the emerging technological world we are living in today. I urge everyone to take the time to stay current with the trends these technologies are on, and where they lead as they are the keys to the future – not only of technology, but the future of society, our environment, and our universe as we know it.

Notes

Part 1 – Cyber Security

Dawn of the Code War: America's Battle Against Russia, China, and the Rising Global Cyber Threat

Book by Garrett Graff and John P. Carlin

Cybersecurity Law

Book by Jeff Kosseff

The Art of Deception

Book by Kevin Mitnick and William L. Simon

Cybersecurity and Cyberwar: What Everyone Needs to Know

Book by Allan Friedman and P. W. Singer

Part 2 – Internet of Things

Designing the Internet of Things

Book by Adrian McEwen and Hakim Cassimally

Internet of Things: A Hands-on Approach

Book by Arshdeep Bahga and Vijay K. Madisetti

Rethinking the Internet of Things: A Scalable Approach to Connecting Everything

Book by Francis daCosta

IoT Fundamentals: Networking Technologies, Protocols, and Use Cases for the Internet of Things

Book by Gonzalo Salgueiro and Patrick Grossetete

https://www.i-scoop.eu/internet-of-things-guide/internet-of-things-in-manufacturing/

https://www.newgenapps.com/blog/8-uses-applications-and-benefits-of-industrial-iot-in-manufacturing

https://www.manufacturing.net/article/2018/07/connection-between-smart-manufacturing-and-iot

https://www.cybertalk.org/2018/10/09/new-legislation-holds-manufacturers-responsible-for-iot-cybersecurity/

https://internetofthingsagenda.techtarget.com/feature/ Explained-What-is-the-Internet-of-Things

https://www.sas.com/en_us/whitepapers/non-geek-a-to-z-guideto-internet-of-things-108846.html?utm_source=google&utm_medium=cpc&utm_campaign=iot-us&utm_content=GMS-57027&keyword=internet+of+things&matchtype=p&publisher=google&gclid=Cj0KCQjwi8fdBRCVARIsAEk-Dvnly_TQbu31MPUEnxYsMGbgBO7o817xsJAp0M7dWJAnk779MKAAVT-NYaAq6DEALw_wcB

https://www.coindesk.com/information/what-is-blockchain-technology/

https://www.iotforall.com/what-is-iot-simple-explanation/ https://jaxenter.

com/iot-cyber-security-143871.html

https://www.csoonline.com/article/3244467/internet-of-things/2018-prediction-securing-iot-connected-devices-will-be-a-major-cybersecurity-challenge.html

https://internetofthingsagenda.techtarget.com/blog/IoT-Agenda/ How-IoT-is-reshaping-the-cybersecurity-landscape

https://mapr.com/blog/the-challenge-of-cybersecurity-in-iot-andwhat-you-can-do-about-it

Part 3 – Blockchain

Blockchain: Blueprint for a New Economy by Melanie Swan

Blockchain Revolution: How the Technology Behind Bitcoin Is Changing Money, Business, and the World

Book by Alex Tapscott and Don Tapscott

Blockchain Technology Explained: The Ultimate Beginner's Guide Book by Alan T. Norman

https://blog.capterra.com/benefits-of-blockchain-cybersecurity/ https://www.clickatell.com/articles/information-security/ blockchain-cybersecurity/ https://www.coindesk.com/information/what-is-block-chain-technology https://medium.com/the-mission/a-simple-explana-tion-on-howblockchain-works-e52f75da6e9a

https://www.linkedin.com/pulse/blockchain-cybersecuri-ty-what-you-need-know-avoid-david/?fbclid=IwAR03w95YXkUNsdM-Crd-MF77N3doHG_x3DTPhO7ujgwEPlIGJf7L-V3Sf9m8 https://bitcoinist.com/imf-lagarde-state-digital-currencies/?fbclid=IwAR0FD9hjN1xK0hOtohg-6Z7YQ_cFepv-Pjiixx3055h7eTkm7udREqgx0UIo

Part 4 – Artificial Intelligence

Introduction to Artificial Intelligence

Book by Philip C. Jackson

Machine Learning and Security: Protecting Systems with Data and Algo-rithms

Book by Clarence Chio and David Freeman

Artificial Intelligence Tools for Cyber Attribution

by Eric Nunes, Paulo Shakarian, Gerardo I. Simari, Andrew Ruef

CPSIA information can be obtained
at www.ICGtesting.com
Printed in the USA
LVHW081205280119
605485LV00010B/228/P